Dear Mad'm

Who Was She?

Peter Walthall Lismer
and
Elizabeth Kellam Lismer

Naturegraph Publishers

Library of Congress Cataloging-in-Publication Data

Lismer, Peter Walthall, 1937-

Dear Mad'm, who was she? / Peter Walthall Lismer and Elizabeth Kellam Lismer.

    p. cm.

ISBN 978-0-87961-281-8

1. Patterson, Stella Walthall, 1866-1955. 2. Women pioneers--California--Biography. 3. Pioneers--California--Biography. 4. Storytellers--California--Biography. 5. Artists--California--Biography. 6. California--Biography. 7. Mountain life--California--History. 8. Klamath River Valley (Or. and Calif.)--Biography. 9. Klamath River Valley (Or. and Calif.)--Social life and customs. I. Lismer, Elizabeth Kellam. II. Title.

CT275.P465L57 2012

920.72--dc23

[B]

Copyright © 2012
by Peter Walthall Lismer and Elizabeth Kellam Lismer

Cover illustrators: Alice Harvey and Vivian Witt

Naturegraph Publishers has been publishing books on natural history, Native Americans, and outdoor subjects since 1946. Free catalog available.

Books for a better world

Naturegraph Publishers, Inc.
PO Box 1047 ● 3543 Indian Creek Rd.
Happy Camp, CA 96039
(530) 493-5353
www.naturegraph.com

Stella Patterson at her mining claim.   Pioneer Press

We dedicate this book
to our parents and grandparents,
who showed us how
to grow old gracefully,
and especially to Stella,
who proved that
even though you grow older,
you don't have to lose your
spirit of adventure.

Table of Contents

Part Two

Acknowledgements

This book would not have been possible without the help of an army of people that we have dubbed "Friends of Stella." Invoking the name, Stella Walthall Patterson, was like saying "Open Sesame!" Everyone we have met during the last six years has been so enthusiastic about our project, and so helpful in our research, that we were constantly encouraged to keep moving forward. We have not found out everything that we would like to know, but we have gotten a good picture of who Stella was.

We would never have started to write this book if Barbara Brown at Naturegraph Publishers had not asked us to do it. We met Barbara on a trip to Happy Camp, and she showed us her folder of fan letters asking for more information about Stella. She said that since we were researching anyway, would we consider writing a short book? That was the beginning of our six-year search.

Many people in Happy Camp have shared information, pictures, and their time with us. We are very grateful to Marguerite Connor, Kathi Jones, Pauline Attebery, Roberta Everett, Judy Bushy, and Karen Tulledo for all their help. Also, we appreciate the cooperation of the Happy Camp Chamber of Commerce, Skip Davis and others at the Happy Camp Ranger Station, Klamath National Forest, and of the denizens of the Frontier Café.

Willow Creek was very important to our story, and Margaret Wooden and everyone at the Willow Creek – China Flat Museum was extremely helpful. Margaret was very generous in sharing her time and knowledge with us. Donna Ammon followed up after a phone call to her and put us in touch with Kim Kelsey, who generously shared information about her brother, Stanley Patterson.

In Redding, Hazel Gendron and Edward Cooper Waterman spent time with us and gave us a lot of information. As a teenager, Mr. Waterman worked on the Patterson Ranch, and so he knew Jim, Stella, and Ralph Patterson, as well as Fred Crooks and Cy Jensen. His personal memories gave us a much richer picture than we could have otherwise gotten.

In Arcata, we met a whole group of people who dedicate their lives to history and the search for knowledge. Edie Butler in the Humboldt Room at Humboldt State University was especially helpful. After she had helped us navigate their extensive collection, she invited us back for another visit to go to the Phillips House Museum in Arcata, because she remembered, being the volunteer archivist for the Historical Sites Society of Arcata, that the Horel/Caskey Collection contained diaries in which Stella and Jim Patterson were mentioned. What a treasure trove of information they provided!

Janet Eidsness, Valerie Budig-Markin, and Gay Berrien were all very helpful in locating information. To Gay, a special thanks for arranging with the Trinity County Historical Society for the use of the picture of Stella and Jim that was taken shortly after their marriage by Nellie Ladd.

The Mills College Alumnae Association and Mills Archivist Janis Braun provided invaluable information about Stella's years at Mills, both as a student and as a teaching assistant. We also wish to acknowledge the editing done by Jessica Young and the Editing for Publication course at Chico State University.

We were very happy to meet Thelma and Everett Doutt's grandson, Bill, his wife, Theresa, and their daughter during our search for information, and we hope to see them again.

Another group of people who have not only provided lots of information about Stella and Jim and their lives, but who have also enriched ours, is the Covert-Walthall-Patterson clan. Covert descendents, Rod Diridon Sr. and his wife, Dr. Gloria Duffy; Claudia Diridon Wagner and her husband, Dick; Kathy Covert Yawn; and Sheila Murphy Pickwell have all provided much support and encouragement, as have Jim Patterson's great-niece, Cindy Trobitz-Thomas and her husband, Vince. We are very happy to have these "new" relatives in our lives, and we would probably never have met them without Stella's influence.

Another Covert descendent, Clayton Willms, deserves a special thanks. Clayton's grandparents were David and Wasson Covert Rickart, and they were the ones who raised Stella's brother Mat. Because of that, Mat, and after his death, his wife, Alice Walthall Peck, and his daughter, Sydney Walthall Lismer, remained very close to the Willms family. Clayton gave us two of Stella's paintings and several pictures from his family album. Clayton was always a generous and loving man. He passed away in 2008 at the age of ninety-four.

Last, but certainly not least, we thank our family and friends for their support and encouragement as we have been working on this book. Karen Dolder came to the rescue on some English grammar questions, and we would especially like to thank our daughter-in-law, Melissa Kincaid, for her help in reading and editing. We really appreciate the time and thought put into it.

If we have inadvertently overlooked anyone, please forgive us, as after six years of working on this project, our brains are overtaxed and need a rest.

Elizabeth Kellam Lismer

Peter Walthall Lismer

Prologue

Living with my grandmother and mother, I (Peter talking here) do not remember ever hearing anything about my grandaunt Stella until I was an adult and my mother showed me her book. Even then, I wasn't told very much about her, other than she was my grandfather's sister. Years later, when I married Elizabeth and she became interested in my family history, we finally read the book. After reading *Dear Mad'm*, we, like so many others, had a million questions about Stella Walthall Belcher Patterson. Who was she? What was she like? How did a woman, born in 1866 and orphaned when quite young, do all of the things she did? We began to look for answers, and with the help of many other "Friends of Stella," we hope we will be able to shed some light on an absolutely fascinating woman. Although there are areas of her life that are still a mystery to us, we have no doubt that she enriched not only the lives of those who were fortunate enough to know her, but also of those of us who have read her works.

Much of our impression of Stella Patterson comes from her own writings—short stories, *Dear Mad'm*, of course, and also letters that were kept in the family and at Mills College. We have also spoken with people who knew her and have used information from newspapers and other printed materials. We have searched for several years to find out as much as we can, and that research has taken us from San Francisco; to the Central Valley; to the mountains of Northern California; to Paris, France.

We discovered that among all of the things Stella was— teacher, artist, pianist, writer, wife, mother, adventurer—one thing stands out above everything else. Stella was a storyteller. She loved to tell a good story and could hold her listeners spellbound as she wove a tale.[1] Her first story was published at age fourteen and her last was *Dear Mad'm*, published just after her death. Stella was scheduled to be the guest speaker for the Mills College graduation of June 1956, but she died in December of 1955. Mills's President White based his remarks to the graduating class that year on her. He said:

> It is very hard to say good-bye to a graduating class without seeming a bit maudlin. The faculty, the trustees, and I wish so much for each of you, and we have such confidence in you. We wish you challenging jobs, worthy husbands, and affectionate children. But above all we wish you qualities of life, which it is harder to put into words. What I mean is illustrated by a member of the old Mills Seminary class of 1883—she graduated two years before Mills College started. Her name was Mrs. Stella Walthall Patterson. On this campus, living in Mills Hall, she got interested in writing, and in the observation of life, which is the foundation of good writing. In 1882, while still in the seminary, she published her first short story in the *Oakland Tribune*, no less. She continued writing, contributing to some of the country's best magazines, mixing with the vivid literary life of San Francisco at the turn of the century.
>
> She was already forty when the earthquake and fire of 1906 destroyed everything she had. She moved to Yreka north of Mount Shasta, lived quietly and continued to write. Then at the age of eighty she moved again to live alone in a lonely cabin in the Siskiyou Mountains on the banks of the Klamath.
>
> This spring of 1956, she died, at the age of ninety, having just completed an extraordinary book, *Dear Mad'm*, published a month ago by W.W. Norton. (Authors' note: She actually died in December of 1955 at age eighty-nine.) The reviewers have invariably said that your fellow alumna, Mrs. Patterson, is the closest thing to a feminine Thoreau that this country has produced. The book is the reflection of a life simple in external pattern, but thoughtful, close to the ultimate realities.
>
> As the file of her letters in our alumnae office shows, Mrs. Patterson, during all of her life, felt that her intellectual roots were in the soil of this campus. Here she had learned to see and how to share what she saw.
>
> Whether your lives are short or long—and let me assure you that no small number of you will be coming back for reunions

seventy plus years hence whether you live in a Klamath cabin or a city apartment—the things we-who-remain at Mills most wish for you-who-depart are the things which Mrs. Patterson had: intellectuality mellowed by insight; warmth without obsessiveness; compassion without sentimentality; and above all, the dual capacity both for being serenely alone even in a crowd and at the same time for feeling akin to all men even in a wilderness. It is these qualities which we hope each of you may have gained here, at least to some measure.

And so for the faculty, the trustees, and for myself—for all of us who stay—I wish you Godspeed.[2]

In researching for our book, we began to understand who Peter's aunt Stella Burfoot Walthall Belcher Patterson was, as well as some of the other people that she knew, and we began to realize how special they all were. Stella, Fred Crooks, Cy Jenson, Jim Patterson, and others whom you will meet in the following pages, and all those who, in the early part of the twentieth century, left a more comfortable life and went into the mountains to live, survive, and for some, to prosper. They were farmers, hunters and trappers, prospectors, store owners, and dreamers who all loved the wilderness. Many others who came later fled because it was too primitive and they needed more comforts, but those who stayed became a part of the fabric that we know today as early California Pioneers.

As Stella noted in *Dear Mad'm*, when she moved into her cabin she had very little, but she created a new life for herself. She brought seeds, and with those seeds she created a garden and orchard and in doing that, she planted her roots into the soil of the Siskiyous. She also came with her family's love of the mountains. We, today, would say life was very hard then, because they didn't have all of the modern conveniences, such as electricity, plumbing, telephones, television, automobiles, and paved roads. Those pleasures would come to later generations. However, they did have a desire to be comfortable, and as Stella said, she had a warm blanket to snuggle into at night and an outhouse to visit when nature called. At night, she used a lantern or candles to read or write by and a wonderful wood-burning stove to cook on, and she had Vicki, her dog, as companion. With those meager comforts, she was content. She also had "Dear Sir" and "Up'n Up" nearby to help her when needed.

Other than "Dear Sir" and "Up'nUp," we haven't been able to find much information about the other characters in the book, except that they existed. Frenchy lived down river from Stella, and Millicent did live nearby, but we don't know if that was her real name. As for Tom, the mail driver, he may have been a composite of two drivers, or he may have been one of the two. The mail route was divided at some point between two drivers. One took mail toward Yreka and the other toward Willow Creek. Pete Peters drove the mail truck from about 1940 until 1972, and we have heard that he was the one to bring Stella to the claim originally, but we could not verify that.[3] Another driver, whose name we could not find, was a good friend of John and Allie Covert, Stella's cousins and later neighbors, and often stopped by their house for a piece of pie. He was killed when his truck was run off the road in the early 1950s.[4]

"Up'nUp's" name was Clarence "Cy" Jensen. His wife, Norah in the book, did eventually leave the mountains and they divorced. He remarried, this time to a woman from the area. After his death in 1990, at age seventy-eight, he was cremated and his widow eventually scattered his ashes under an apple tree on the claim at Clear Creek, as he had requested.[5]

"Dear Sir," whose real name was Fred Crooks, was well known to residents of Clear Creek and Happy Camp. Fred Crooks remained a devoted friend to Stella throughout her life. He continued to live in the area until his death in 1975, at the age of eight-nine. He is buried in the Happy Camp cemetery.

With all that said, let's go back in time and see who "Dear Mad'm" really was, and hopefully answer questions from her hundreds of fan letters.

Chapter One

Family Background

That Stella Walthall Belcher Patterson was an extraordinary woman there is no doubt. Any woman today who did all of the things that she did would still be unusual, but what gave her the ability to live her life as she chose, especially given that she was born almost one hundred and fifty years ago? What made Stella who she was? Was there something in her background that gave her such an independent spirit? When she was almost seventy, she wrote, "I have none of that let-down feeling that is supposed to come with advancing years. In fact I do not realize that most of my life is behind me. I am as ready for new adventures as a girl."[6] Perhaps a look at the pioneering families that she came from will provide some of the answers.

Both sides of her family came to America in the mid-1600s. The Coverts, her maternal ancestors, came from Holland to New Amsterdam (later, New York) in 1650. They were probably French Huguenots. From Brooklyn, they went to New Jersey, then on to Indiana, and then to Ozark, Arkansas, where Stella's mother, Sarah Emeline Covert, was born in 1846. In 1838, Sarah's father, John Bates Covert went with John C. Fremont to California, later returning to his home in Arkansas. In 1856, he again left Arkansas for California with his family, including seven of his eight children, and crossed the plains in an ox team train of forty wagons, also bringing with them a lot of cattle. Six months were necessary to complete the journey, which they accomplished safely, coming by the way of Salt Lake City.[7] Stella's grandfather John Bates Covert bought a ranch near Stockton and began farming again. The Covert's oldest son, Luke, was already married and stayed in Arkansas. During the Civil War, he served in the Confederate Army, was captured in Little Rock, Arkansas, and sadly, died in a prisoner of war camp in Indiana in 1864.

The Walthalls, Stella's paternal ancestors, were Welsh and came via England to Virginia around 1645. They settled on "Royal Patent Land," near Appomattox. The area they settled was called Port Walthall. In 1793, Stella's great-grandfather, John Walthall, married Catherine Madison, a cousin of President James Madison. Their son, Stella's grandfather, Madison Walthall, married Elizabeth Frances Burfoot in 1834, after the death of his first wife, and they began their migration westward. Elizabeth also came from an old Virginia family. Her grandfather, Thomas Burfoot, was a lieutenant in the Revolutionary War who received a land grant in Chesterfield County, Virginia, for his service. This connection allowed Stella to join the Daughters of the American Revolution in the 1890s.[8] Madison and Elizabeth moved to Columbus, Mississippi, after their marriage. In Mississippi, Madison was a busy man! He bought a lot of land, served as president of the Real Estate Bank, and was on the first board of trustees for the Mississippi Female College.[9] He served as a captain in the Mexican War in a Mississippi rifle regiment raised by Jefferson Davis and fought at the battle of Buena Vista in February 1847.[10]

After the war, in 1848, Madison went to California and settled in the Stockton area, in a town called Walthall, which no longer exists. Madison served in California's territorial legislature and was one of the three assemblymen to sign the petition to Congress requesting statehood for California.[11] While in the legislature, as the new county lines for the state were being drawn, Madison proposed the name of Shasta for that county, and it was adopted. He was also the first tax collector for the Port of Stockton.[12] In 1853, Madison was one of the founding members, and was a trustee, of the First Baptist Church in Stockton, California.[13]

In 1856, Madison, originally a southern Democrat, was instrumental in organizing the new Republican Party in San Joaquin County. Their resolutions in part declared, "that the Republican Party is organized to preserve the liberties of the people, the sovereignty of states, and the perpetuity of the Union." They adopted the principle of the prohibition of slavery in all national territories and the prevention of the increase of the political power of slavery. Slavery, they declared, is "a sectional institution in which only about 350,000 slaveholders are directly interested, while freedom is a national principle by which 26,000,000 of American freemen are secured in their rights."[14] Madison was elected secretary of the first San Joaquin County Republican convention, which nominated John C. Fremont for president of the United States.[15] In February 1861, Madison "on his farm, hoisted a bear flag, and the *Argus* [a newspaper] called him a 'disunionist.' This epithet offended Mr. Walthall and in a newspaper card he declared: 'I can say we are not disunionists. Everybody knows what the bear flag means. It means that when the Union is dissolved we intend to be independent—not before.'"[16] Very interesting for a man who had been raised in Virginia, lived in Mississippi, fought with Jefferson Davis in the Mexican War, and who had owned slaves himself in both Virginia and Mississippi. Madison was the oldest of six surviving brothers. Three brothers stayed in Virginia, one went to Iowa, one to Mississippi, and Madison to California after living in Mississippi. It would be interesting to know whether he maintained contact with his family, or just went ahead without looking back. Madison left his son from his first marriage, John Bowers Walthall, then age five, in Virginia when he moved to Mississippi. John became a physician and remained in Virginia his whole life. Perhaps they did maintain contact, because when Madison died he left John his full third of the inheritance.[17]

While still in Mississippi, Madison and Elizabeth had two sons, Madison Jr., Stella's father, born in 1836, and Lawson Burfoot, born in 1844. After he had established himself in California, Madison Sr. returned to Mississippi, and he and

Stella Burfoot Walthall's Family Tree

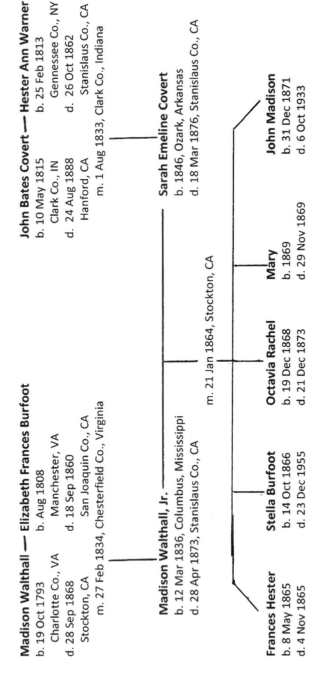

Madison Walthall, Sr.,
mid-1800s Lismer Family

Elizabeth Burfoot Walthall, circa
1850 Lismer Family

Madison Walthall, Jr., circa 1860s
Lismer Family, from Clayton Willms

Sarah Covert Walthall, circa 1870
Lismer Family , from Clayton Willms

Elizabeth and the two boys crossed the Isthmus of Panama and arrived in California on the ship *Columbus* on May 23, 1851.

In 1859, at age fifteen, Lawson, called L.B., was sent to Richmond, Virginia, to attend the Baptist College. Then he went to North Carolina to an uncle, and attended the Beulah Male Institute for one year. When the Civil War broke out, he served behind the lines in a North Carolina regiment of the Confederate Army from April 1861 to July 1862, as one-year conscriptions were common at the beginning of the war. L.B. was eighteen years old when he left the army. In 1863, he went to New York City, and finally returned to California on March 1, 1864, at the age of twenty.[18] What mixed feelings he must have had about the war since he had family members on both sides of the conflict!

Stella's parents, Madison Walthall Jr. (March 12, 1836–April 28, 1873) and Sarah Emeline Covert (1846–March 18, 1876) were married January 21, 1864 when he was twenty-seven and she seventeen. It was a double ceremony with Sarah's sister Rose Covert and Franklin Davis. Madison and Sarah had five children, but only Stella, born October 14, 1866, and her brother, John Madison, born December 31, 1871, survived.

Madison Jr. farmed with his father in the Stockton area, but was also actively engaged in surveying throughout California and was for some years employed in a land office and the real estate business.[19] He was a member of the Pioneer Society, formed in 1869, which included the wealthiest and most influential men in the county.[20] Unfortunately, he contracted pneumonia and died in 1873 at the age of thirty-seven. Sarah Covert Walthall, who had come overland to California with her family in 1856 when she was ten years old, died in 1876 at the age of thirty.

Stella wrote that she was orphaned at the age of seven, in 1873, which is odd, because that is when her father died, but her mother lived another three years. It is unknown why Stella and John Madison, who was called Mat, were not taken care of by their mother while she remained alive. Perhaps she was either physically or emotionally unable to care for them. Sarah's daughter Octavia, born in 1869, died in December 1873, the same year as her father, Madison Jr. Octavia was the third child of theirs to die. What tragedy Sarah had within a few short years! On March 3, 1874, Sarah wrote her will in which she made L. B. Walthall, her brother-in-law, the "immediately appointed guardian" for the children. She also asked to have her husband and three children's remains moved to the Linden Cemetery. Sarah died in March 1876. Her place of death and burial site are unknown, but she is not buried in the Linden Cemetery with her parents, husband, and three children. It is a mystery! Probate records show that her estate was valued at $9,000–10,000 at the time of her death, so there were some funds left to care for the children.

Stella referred to L.B. Walthall as her "bachelor uncle." He had been married, in 1869, to Sarah's first cousin, but was a widower when he became the children's guardian. He remarried in 1877. Mat, who was just two when his father died, was raised by one of Sarah's sisters and her husband until he went to a prep school as a teenager. Why wasn't Stella taken into one of her relatives' families? Instead, she was put into a number of different boarding schools, until she and her uncle settled on Mills Seminary in Oakland, California. Perhaps that was the beginning of her acquiring her spirit of self-reliance and independence?

In spite of growing up separately most of their lives, Stella and Mat had a very close relationship. Mat spent all of his life in California and was a truly devoted son of the state. When he was two years old, he went to live outside of Modesto on the ranch of his maternal aunt and uncle, David and Ora Wasson Covert Rickart. After the lower grammar grades, he attended the Atascadero Military Academy, then graduated from the University of California where he played football for three years, earning his Big C varsity letter. He studied law at Hastings Law School in San Francisco, graduating in 1898. He became a member of the California Bar and returned to live and practice in Modesto. He was always proud of Modesto and was vitally concerned with its development. He was one of the early district attorneys in Modesto and later was attorney for the Southern Pacific Railroad, in addition to having his own practice. His office was above the Modesto Bank. Mat joined with several other Modesto men and formed the original golf club in Modesto. For many years, his fondest relaxation was golf and all activities involved in the development of the new club. He was a member of the Rotary Club, the Elks Club, the Chamber of Commerce, and the Masonic Lodge. He was also an officer in the National Guard unit of Stanislaus County. Mat married Alice Atwood in 1907 and they had one daughter, Sidney, born October 4, 1911. Sidney's only child, Peter Walthall Lismer, is one of the authors of this book.

Mat had a deep and absorbing interest in and knowledge of the geology and history of California, which prompted many wonderful trips with his family. Once he walked from Yosemite Valley to Lake Tahoe with a group of men so that he could see first hand that nearly inaccessible area. He, as the landowner's attorney, helped start the resort area known as Twain Harte. In fact, it was he who gave Twain Harte its name and helped develop its first golf course and the small lake. All his life he found rest and strength from spending just a few hours walking through a field or on the mountain trails. Both Mat and Stella learned to understand and love the quiet of the open country and this never left either of them.

Like Stella, Mat was also a very fine artist. He mostly used pen and ink and was a caricaturist who continually made sketches of his friends, people involved in his court cases, and people he saw during his trips throughout Europe and California. He had a beautiful baritone voice, and, when younger, was a member of the early Modesto singing and players group. He helped to design and paint scenery and costumes for many of the light operas and plays that were produced.[21] Apparently, talent ran in the family!

With an understanding of where Stella came from, it's no wonder she was an adventurous soul! Let's see where she went from there.

Stella Burfoot Walthall, early 1870s   Lismer Family

John Madison and Stella Walthall, early 1870s
Lismer Family

Chapter Two

The Education of "Dear Mad'm"

Stella lived in Stockton until she was seven years old. After her father died, she began attending boarding schools. Apparently, the first several were either not to her liking or to her uncle's, because they tried several before settling on Mills Seminary in the Oakland hills in 1878.

In "A Brief Autobiography" which Stella wrote two months before her death, she gives the following account of her time at Mills.

> Up to this time I had managed to elude about everything in the way of education, but Mrs. Mills took me in hand, put me in the Mills preparatory school, and strongly advised me to apply myself to the three R's. I really studied after that to please Mrs. Mills, whom I really loved, and was able to enter the regular Seminary course when I was thirteen. But learning still didn't appeal to me and I spent most of my time browsing in the "Bryant Library" or writing fearful and shocking stories of my own invention. I sent one of these effusions to the *Oakland Tribune* when I was fourteen. It was accepted, printed, and paid for along with an encouraging letter from the editor, but my English teachers, they were chagrined at my grammatical errors, lack of punctuation, etc.
>
> When I was sixteen, I found myself in the senior class and all primed to graduate in the Class of '83. Mr. and Mrs. Mills called me and others of the class to a solemn meeting in their study. After prayer and a brief talk, Mr. Mills turned to me and said pointedly, "In Honolulu, we'd have called you a smoked banana." Then he and Mrs. Mills laughed heartily.

Stella Burfoot Walthall, early 1880s   Lismer Family

We teenagers were shocked. We didn't know these two good people could laugh. Mr. Mills continued, "We have decided to let you graduate if you will promise us to return and enter Mills College when it opens." I gave my promise and kept it, although I never finished my college course. I was a student teacher. For three years I was Professor Lisser's assistant, having a large class of beginners on the piano and continuing my lessons with Professor Lisser. After five or more hours daily teaching and four—often five—hours of grilling work on the piano to please my teacher, I had little time left for any college studies. I did make a "pass" at French, Latin, and English, but all was spasmodic." [22]

A smoked banana referred to bananas which were shipped green from the islands and then yellowed by oven processing so that they looked ripe but weren't![23]

Stella was greatly influenced by Mrs. Mills. In 1945, she was asked to contribute her memories of Mrs. Mills for a biography that was being written about her by Professor E. O. James of the Mills faculty.

Stella had intended to write an "unforgettable character" sketch about Mrs. Mills, but said that she had more than she could do with other work and would be glad indeed to turn over her material to Mr. James.[24] Josephine Brizard Appleton, a family friend, also wrote, "Mrs. P said that in her oppinion [sic] Mrs. D's description of Mrs. Mills [sic] regal walk, hardly described it. She bounced, rather Patty [Stella Patterson] says, and delighted mother and me by illustrating just what she meant by bouncing! She evidently has a most vivid memory and is as young in spirit and as peppy as if she were still a school girl."[25] Stella remained proud of Mills and her association with it, and was a life-long member of its alumnae association. She contributed money from time to time for various projects[26] and was very pleased to be asked to speak to the graduating class of 1956 after *Dear Mad'm* was published. Unfortunately, her death made that impossible, as was noted earlier.

After her three years teaching and studying at Mills,[27] Stella spent a year as a teacher at the Field Seminary in Oakland,[28] and then, sometime in 1888 or 1889, came the opportunity to go to Paris. What an exciting time that would have been to be in Paris! The World's Fair, which ran from May through October of 1889, featured the new Eiffel Tower as its entrance archway. All of Paris was abuzz about Mr. Eiffel's tower. There was great debate about whether the tower was a work of art or an eyesore, blighting the city. During its construction there was a letter of protest published in one of the newspapers that was signed by many of the famous artists, musicians, and writers of the day, including Charles Gounod, Alexandre Dumas, Guy de Maupassant, and Charles Garnier, to name just a few. The letter protested "against the erection in the very heart of the capital of the useless and monstrous Eiffel Tower," and they compared it to a gigantic black factory chimney. They even said that the shadow cast over the city would be like an odious dark ink stain! Gustave Eiffel responded that the tower would have her own beauty, that engineers also consider the artistic in their work, and that works can be both durable and elegant.[29] Who would have guessed that the Eiffel Tower would become recognized the world over as the iconic symbol of Paris, La Grande Dame?

The art scene in Paris, while always in the avant-garde, was in a particularly interesting and exciting era. Beyond the Impressionist movement, and into the Post-Impressionists, Paris was teeming with artists who are now considered among the greats—Van Gogh, Gauguin, Seurat, Toulouse-Lautrec, Renoir. It was into this atmosphere that Stella came to study art. "There I really got down to the business of learning. I attended lectures on French literature at the Sorbonne—when possible—studied art at the Delacluse Atelier six days in the week and trying to catch up my education like a starving woman, grasping hungrily at everything where I could learn something."[30] The Delacluse Atelier was located in the Montparnasse area and was regarded as one of the leading edge studios of the day.[31] Stella continued to paint throughout her lifetime. Of her paintings that survive, the

Stella Burfoot Walthall, circa 1890   Lismer Family

influence of the Impressionists can be seen in both technique and subject matter.

Shocking her family with her new habit of smoking,[32] Stella returned to San Francisco in the "Gay Nineties" and taught music at the Van Ness Seminary.[33] In 1892, she participated in a piano recital at the seminary, playing "Spinnerlied" by Wagner-Liszt.[34] On the original dust jacket for *Dear Mad'm* she says, "After studying in Europe I returned to California and led a gay social life in San Francisco, belonging to the literary set and basking in the light of Jack London, Ambrose Bierce, and other writers. I wrote stories for *Century Magazine, Collier's,* and others." It was in this setting that she met her first husband, Edward A. Belcher.

Stella and John Madison Wathall , circa 1890   Lismer Family

Chapter Three

Marriage to Judge Edward A. Belcher

Edward Augustus Belcher was born in August of 1848 in Vermont, possibly the last of at least eleven children. Belcher's father, Samuel, and his first wife, Anna, had seven children. After Anna's death, Samuel married Adeline Experience Dunn, and Edward was their fourth child. Samuel was sixty years old when Edward was born and Adeline forty. The Belchers belonged to one of the oldest families in New England, and Edward was a direct descendant from Jonathan Belcher, who was the colonial governor of Massachusetts and New Hampshire, and later New Jersey. Governor Belcher was also the founder of Princeton College in New Jersey. It is even said that the coat of arms of the United States of America was taken from the coat of arms of the Belcher family![35]

Edward's father was a farmer in Vermont. Edward finished his education at Putnam College and in 1868 followed his two older half-brothers to California. His brothers, William Caldwell Belcher and Isaac Sawyer Belcher, were partners in a law practice in Marysville, California, and urged Edward to come study law with them, which he did. He was admitted to the bar in 1876 and was appointed city attorney of the city of Marysville the following year.[36] Both William and Isaac were very prominent lawyers, both were judges, and Isaac was a state Supreme Court justice for the last twelve years of his life. William remained in practice in Marysville and in San Francisco until his death in 1895. He was very active in the Masonic Lodge, the Scottish Rite, and various other organizations.[37] Isaac and his family also moved to

San Francisco, where they led a very active social life. His estate was valued at $100,000.00 at the time of his death, and included cash, stocks, their residence in San Francisco, and property in four other counties.[38]

Edward practiced law in Marysville and also served in the National Guard. In 1880, he received a commission as aide-de-camp, with the rank of lieutenant colonel, on the staff of Governor Perkins.[39] He served in that capacity until 1882. In June of 1883, he married Katherine Dooley, who was from a pioneer family in Marysville, but the marriage didn't last long, and they were divorced. They had one son, Paul William Belcher, who later became a successful mechanical engineer. Edward and Paul did not have a close relationship, and Edward specifically excluded Paul from his will, leaving everything to his nieces and nephews instead.[40] Paul lived in Salt Lake City until his death, at age fifty-two, in 1936.

In 1884, Edward moved to San Francisco and began to practice law there. He joined the newly formed Dirigo Club and served as its vice president for several terms and composed the "Dirigo March" for the club in 1884. He and several others organized the Union League Club of San Francisco, a Republican club, and he became its first vice president. Edward was also a life member of the Masons.[41]

We do not know how Stella and Edward first met, but it was most likely within the social circles of San Francisco. Stella taught at the Van Ness Academy after her return from Paris, and Edward was practicing law. Despite the great difference in their ages, they seemed to have a number of interests in common, such as their musical abilities and a love of dogs and the great outdoors. When Stella was twenty-six and Edward forty-four, they were married on April 3, 1893 in Modesto, California, and began their married life living on Haight Street in San Francisco. According to the San Francisco Blue Book City Directories, they lived at five different addresses in San Francisco between 1893 and 1905. Edward was appointed judge of the San Francisco Superior Court in October of 1893, not long after their marriage.[42] Their social

Stella in her wedding dress, 1893   Kathi Jones

life was apparently very full. For example, Stella is listed as a guest at the reception showing off the new "home" of the Sorosis Club in 1895. The club was "instituted for the association of women interested in literary, scientific, and philanthropic pursuits, with a view of rendering them helpful to each other, and useful to society." Stella's sister-in-law, Isaac Belcher's wife, was a vice-president of the Sorosis Club. Other well-known members were luminaries such as Mrs. George Crocker, Mrs. Phoebe Hearst, and Mrs. H.E. Huntington.[43] Sometime during their marriage, Stella joined the Daughters of the American Revolution, based on the military service of her great-great-grandfather, Thomas Burfoot.[44]

Stella Walthall Belcher, mid-1890s   Lismer Family

Stella had a life-long love of animals, which is apparent to all readers of *Dear Mad'm*. Her last faithful companion, Vicki, the border collie, features prominently in that story, along with Pete the mule, and all the goats. Stella and Edward had a dog named Chum who was also obviously well loved, according to the quantity of pictures that were taken of him. Stella wrote many short stories for various publications during their marriage, a number of which can still be found today. Several of them also feature animals as main characters, including a rooster, a polar bear cub, and a Chihuahua. Her story "A Fatal Climax," which was published in *Century Magazine* in 1896, is included on Cornell University's website in their Making of America series.

Edward and Stella's appreciation of the outdoors, and their many friends and family, caused them to travel quite a bit around California. A family photo album records some of those travels and includes clever comments written by the judge, which show that he, as well as Stella, had a good sense of humor. Their travels took them to Yosemite, Highland Springs, the Santa Cruz mountains, Mount Tamalpais, Clear Lake, and a number of places in the Mount Shasta region, including Castle Crags and the fish hatchery at Sisson. There are a number of pictures from July 1900 of Edward with some other men who climbed to the top of Mount Shasta. He notes that the round trip took thirteen hours. Also on that same vacation, they were staying at Castle Crags when a large fire broke out in which the annex to the tavern burned down. Other activities shown in the album were walking/running races at Blythedale, walking in the hills above Mill Valley, and golfing in Marysville where they went to visit Edward's nephew Richard Belcher. In 1903, they went north to Humboldt County and took pictures on the Hoopa Indian reservation of Captain John's sweat house. Captain John would later be featured in a short story that Stella wrote, called "God's Way." Also on that trip, they photographed Jeremiah "Jere" Smith, a well-known rancher in the area, who will be discussed in the next chapter.

Edward developed some health problems, so he took a leave

Stella and Edward A. Belcher, 1890   Lismer Family

of absence from the bench, and he and Stella went to live in Arcata for a year or so in 1905 so that he could recuperate. They had friends there, and the mountain air was said to have been responsible for restoring his health.[45]

According to a variety of sources, it was on one of these trips up north that Stella and Edward met a young guide named Jim Patterson.[46] No real details have come to light, but apparently Jim and Stella fell in love. Stella then went to Maricopa County in the Arizona territory so that she could obtain a divorce from Judge Belcher without having any mention of it in the San Francisco papers.[47] She had to live there for more than one year in order to establish residency before the divorce could be finalized. It was final on December 19, 1906, which means that Stella was not in San Francisco in April of 1906 during the infamous

Sam Mitchell and Edward A. Belcher at Dutch Flat, 1911
Lismer Family

earthquake that destroyed many of her personal belongings. The final divorce papers show that during that year Stella lived without any support from Edward.

Judge Belcher continued to live and work in San Francisco. His last residence is shown as the Union League Club. He did not remarry. On December 17, 1928, while crossing the street, a cable car ran into him and he died of the accident two days later, age eighty. He was cremated and buried at Woodlawn Cemetery in San Mateo, California. His probate file shows that the California Street Cable RR Company paid

$360.80 for funeral expenses and for injury to the deceased. What a sad end for a man of such talent and vigor. Whether Stella knew of his misfortune or not, we'll never know. By the time of Edward's death, she was well established in her mountain life with Jim Patterson. More adventures were yet to come!

***Stella Walthall Belcher,
late 1890s***   Lismer Family

Chapter Four

Marriage to James B. Patterson

James Benjamin Patterson, known to his friends and family as Jim, was also from a family of early pioneers. His great-grandfather had migrated from Vermont to New York, where Jim's grandfather, Azel S. Patterson, was born in 1824. The family then went to Illinois, where Azel met and married Mary Wilson, whose family had come there from Ohio. Azel and Mary settled in California sometime before the birth of their first son, William, who was born in 1853. Azel may have been in California earlier, along with his brother Moses, for the Gold Rush in 1850. James Henry Patterson, Jim's father, born in 1855, was the second of ten children. Jim's mother, Ludvina Barboni, came from Switzerland. She and her daughter Celeste arrived in New York in 1881. What route she took to get to California is unknown, but she and James Henry were married in California in 1882. James Henry and Ludvina had two sons, James Benjamin, born on April 30, 1883, and Fred Henry, in May of 1884. Then came three daughters, Lodovina, born in 1885; Grace, in 1887; and Eva, in 1889. The Pattersons built a farm about seven miles above the mouth of New River, in Trinity County, California. It was covered with oak and was considered a fine farm, with ample water for irrigation. It was noted that they welcomed travelers overnight.[48] Jim would later continue, on his own ranch, the pattern that his parents set for hospitality, but that's getting ahead of the story.

Sometime between 1901 and 1905, Jim left his parents' ranch and went to work for Jere Smith on his ranch at

Hawkins Bar, also in Trinity County. Jere is described as follows:

> Jeremiah "Jere" Smith had purchased the Hawkins Bar Placer, Hawkins Bar Hydraulic Placer and the Martinville Placer, totaling about three hundred and forty acres, at a sheriff's sale in 1885 after the previous owners had let the operation go.
>
> Smith had access to a water-powered sawmill on Hawkins Creek that made lumber for flumes and buildings…. He was a farmer at heart and developed his property into a beautiful agricultural area. He had three orchards with a total of two hundred and fifty trees, hay fields, pasture, a large garden spot, and a small vineyard…. Smith's establishment was known for hospitality and could be counted on for a meal and overnight lodging. He boarded trail crews and in 1902 boarded a bridge crew that was building the first bridge, a mule bridge, spanning the Trinity River at Hawkins Bar.
>
> Jere lived in a two-room cabin. One room he used for sleeping and the other held his small store. The main building was where the traveling public was entertained, fed, and stayed overnight, with the men utilizing the large upstairs room for sleeping, while women were put up in the downstairs bedrooms…. The "backyard facility" was located a convenient distance away and was used by all. It is not known whether it was a one or two-holer.
>
> Smith and Patterson had their hands full with farm activity. From plowing and seeding grain, to pruning, raising cattle and hogs, and preserving food for winter. There was firewood to cut, split, and haul, work on the trail, and fence building, which included falling a tree that had straight grain suitable for splitting pickets. Their cattle ranged all the way up to Grove's Prairie, working their way down to the ranch during winter. In the spring, when the grass began to grow, the stock would work their way back up the mountain, which meant taking salt to the cattle and checking on their condition.
>
> Pack trains didn't travel in winter into the New River country because of snow and dangerous trail conditions, but during the rest of the year the trail became dusty with the beat of many feet of both man and beast. Miners, mine promoters,

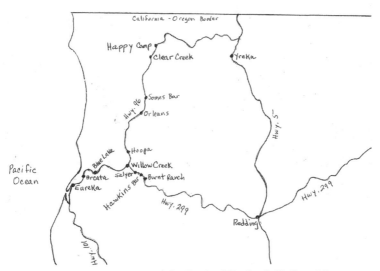

Sketch of Areas Important to Stella, by Elizabeth Kellam Lismer

James Benjamin Patterson, circa 1950? Cindy Trobitz-Thomas

Jeremiah "Jere" Smith, 1903 Lismer Family

mail carriers, and families traveling up and down this main trail into the booming mining country kept Smith and his partner busy preparing food for the travelers and making sure the animals had a place to stay with plenty of feed. With all this activity going on, it's a wonder these two hardy men got as much ranch work done as they did.

Jere Smith died mid-winter of 1921.... Smith had worked hard, provided employment for others, kept a well-known stopping place where he fed and entertained guests and sold supplies from his small store, which had been stocked by the Brizard pack trains. He was known far and wide as a gentleman. What better way for mankind to remember a pioneer of our country?[49]

It is not known exactly when or where Jim and Stella met, but it is likely that it was either at Jere Smith's place or through their mutual friends, the Brizards. Stella and Judge Belcher had made many trips to the rugged northern part of California, including a trip to the Hoopa Valley on the Klamath River, in 1903, where they took a picture of Jere Smith. Later, in 1905, they went to live in Arcata for a year or so in order to improve the judge's health. As stated earlier, it was on one of their trips that they met Jim Patterson, and nature began to take its course.

Jim and Stella were married on February 19, 1907, in Los Angeles, California. A newspaper article, called "A Mountain Romance" gave the following information:

On Tuesday (ed. note, Feb 26, 1907) evening there registered at the Union Hotel, Mr. and Mrs. James C. [sic] Patterson of Hawkins Bar, who arrived at Eureka on the steamer the same day. The couple took the up river train Wednesday morning, on their way to their mountain home at Jere Smith's place in Trinity county, but before leaving it was learned that the bride was none other than the late wife of Judge Edwin [sic] A. Belcher of San Francisco, her maiden name having been Miss Stella Walthall. The lady has many friends of long standing in Arcata, and to say that they were surprised at the news would be putting it mildly. Only a few people here knew that a separation had taken place, that fact having been kept out of the San Francisco papers, the divorce proceedings having been carried on in Arizona, where the lady remained for a year to establish her residence.

The groom is a stalwart and good-looking young mountaineer, who has had charge of the Smith ranch for some years past. His bride has made several trips in the past to Hawkins Bar with her former husband, Judge Belcher, who was in very bad health, and a year in the bracing mountain air completely restored him, and he is now practicing law in

The Pattersons on the Ladd porch in Old Denny, c. 1907
Nellie Ladd Collection, courtesy of the Trinity County Historical Society

San Francisco. Mrs. Patterson is a literary woman of much
ability, and was among the successful competitors in a recent
Colliers contest, having been paid several hundred dollars
for a story entitled "God's Way." It is understood that the lady
is writing a book, founded on life in the mountains and her
return to the log cabin with her youthful husband to live the
simple life, [which] should certainly furnish the necessary
"local color" to make a most interesting romance.[50]

If Jim and Stella's marriage began in an unconventional
manner, perhaps that was foreshadowing the years to come.
Theirs was certainly not a conventional marriage for the
era in which they lived. They were both hard workers, and
their work, especially Stella's teaching, took them away from
home for long periods of time. Whether it was because of
the necessity of earning a living, or the desire to maintain
independence and to cultivate their separate interests, Jim
and Stella spent a fair bit of their married life apart.

Jim did a variety of different things in order to earn a living. In the early years of their marriage, Jim had a ranch
at Hawkins Bar, between Jere Smith's place and the Irving
Ranch.[51] In 1921, he purchased the 280-acre Douglas Ranch
at Willow Creek, where they made their home with the Circle
P as the ranch's brand. Jim raised cattle and hogs, which
he sold to others, including the Hoopa School[52] and Bull's
Meat Market in Arcata.[53] This meant "driving" the animals
over the mountain trails into the city. Jim served as a county
delegate to the State Cattlemen's Convention in Davis and
consulted with other stockmen in the area to improve both
working relations and profits.[54] Jim was always willing to
assist other ranchers. One example was when he helped
another rancher dehorn his cattle.[55] Ranching was not easy
work, and did have its pitfalls. In 1909, a newspaper account
related the following:

James Patterson of Hawkins Bar came near death's door the
other day. It appears that he had a cow and it and his horse
were running at top speed. The cow got ahead of the horse
and in so doing the horse turned a complete somersault...
throwing the rider and stunning him. When he came to his

senses, he was lying between the cow and horse. His wrists were quite badly hurt and he also received some other injuries. After going to the house and getting his wrists bound, he started for Arcata for medical treatment.[56]

It wasn't only for people that the land proved to be harsh. Heavy frost could produce grains that were poisonous to the livestock, and one of Jim's horses and two mules died after eating some frozen wheat or alfalfa. Jim took good care of his animals, and these deaths upset him.[57]

The year 1915 must have been a busy one, as Jim received an $1,800 contract to clear six miles of right of way for a wagon road up the Trinity River,[58] and he resumed operations at his saw mill on Cedar Creek in order to supply lumber for a flume to be built for the Corona del Oro mine.[59] The sawmill was an ongoing operation through the years; it was noted that in 1912 he was sawing lumber to make a dipping trough and smoke house at his ranch,[60] and in 1918 that he was cutting lumber for a home to be built for the Brousse Brizard family.[61]

Jim also led hunting and fishing trips where he served as guide and cook.[62] In the 1920s, Jim supplied bear meat for several years for the annual Alameda Elks banquet. In 1923, he killed a 300-pound black bear that fed over 450 Elks,[63] and in 1926 he sent three bears to Alameda.[64]

In 1925, Jim dug a big irrigation ditch so that he could convert grain land into alfalfa and orchards.[65] He had also planted an orchard on his earlier ranch at Hawkins Bar.[66] For many years, he cut and supplied Christmas trees to various people in the area.[67]

As she had done before her marriage to Judge Belcher, Stella began again to teach school in either Eureka or Arcata, where she roomed with different families, including the Brizards and the Horels.[68] From February 1922 through June 1923 Stella taught at the school in Hawkins Bar, where she received $130 a month for her work.[69]

She was very happy when she found out that she would be teaching in the Willow Creek school for the 1923-1924 school year, as it would mean being at home.[70] We don't know how many years she taught there, but during the 1928-1929 school year, when she was sixty-two, she went almost 600 miles away from home to teach in Coso, Inyo County! She lived in a log house that was seven thousand feet above sea level, surrounded by peaks that were eight to ten thousand feet high. The country was so mountainous that both Stella and her pupils had to ride burros to school. She taught there only one year, and then returned home to Willow Creek to be with her family.[71]

Stella was normally optimistic about life, but in one of her rare "down" periods, she related to her brother Mat how tired she and Jim were. She was happy that Mat and his family were coming for a visit and wrote in June of 1923,

> Jim is gathering cattle to put on the summit. He is very tired and worn but keeps at it. I have just come home & will be here a week & then off to College for six weeks. I am planning to take Ralph [their adopted son] with me and having his tonsils taken out but will send him home to his daddy as soon as he is over the operation. Do plan to meet me in Arcata & bring me home the last week in July. We need you to come. Jim is working himself to death & so am I. And for what? We need some good sane friend to set us right.[72]

In a follow-up letter she wrote, "I'm afraid you can't read this—I am so dreadfully sleepy I can't hold my head up. I have lost so much sleep I can't seem to catch up."[73]

Although they worked very hard, not all of their life was work. They managed to have a social life as well. In addition to welcoming travelers into their home,[74] they enjoyed visiting with friends and having or attending evening entertainments, including music and singing.[75] Stella always enjoyed a concert or the theater, and would go to Arcata or Eureka to see plays or musical concerts, such as *Uncle Tom's Cabin* and the Australian Boys Choir.[76] Jim and Stella also enjoyed having visits with many relatives, including Jim's mother

Mat, Alice and Sidney Walthall with Jim Patterson and unknown, circa 1923   Lismer Family

Front Porch of the Patterson Ranch In Willow Creek, circa 1923
Lismer Family

and sisters,[77] Stella's brother and sister-in-law, and several of her cousins.[78]

The Trinity Journal reported:

> Mr. and Mrs. J.M. Walthall [Stella's brother and his wife] and Mr. and Mrs. W.N. Steele were guests of Mr. and Mrs. J.B. Patterson of Hawkins Bar last week. They motored over 500 miles for the sake of spending the week end of three days with their relatives, and then motored another 500 miles home again. Some ride, that! Both the Walthalls and the Steeles say that the scenery and the air and the good fellowship of Trinity County cannot be beaten and that it is worth the long ride.[79]

Stella and Jim never had their own children, but in about 1912, they took in a six-year-old foster daughter, Thelma Akin, whose mother had died. Thelma had lived with some cousins in Oregon before coming to live with Stella and Jim. She probably lived with them until 1917. In a letter to her daughter Ruth, Mrs. Lois Horel, a friend of Stella's who lived in Arcata, wrote, "Thelma's father has taken her. Mrs. Patterson will feel badly."[80] Thelma and Stella remained very close throughout their lives, and Thelma referred to Stella as

Jim Patterson and Ralph, circa 1919

Cindy Trobitz-Thomas

"Mother." We'll hear more from her later in Jim and Stella's lives.

In January 1919, Stella and Jim adopted a son, James Ralph Warren Patterson, who was born on February 1, 1918. He was called Ralph, after Ralph Bull, a friend of Jim's who owned Bull's Meat Market in Arcata. Ralph's mother and father died in the devastating flu epidemic of 1918, and he was accompanied from San Francisco to Arcata by a nurse.[81] Stella and the baby stayed at the Horels' home in Arcata from January until mid-April before going back to the ranch via auto stage.[82] We don't know very much about Ralph's childhood, but life on a ranch can provide both freedom and hard work. Apparently, Ralph did not like ranch life and didn't want to follow in his father's footsteps as a rancher.[83] In 1926, Stella thought about moving with Ralph back to Modesto, where she was born, and where her brother lived, but she must have changed her mind, because she didn't do it.[84] In 1930, when Ralph was twelve, the family went camping at Trinity Summit for a week during summer vacation.[85] That same fall, Stella made arrangements for Ralph to live in Arcata so that he could enter the College Training School.[86]

Ralph loved cars and worked driving logging trucks and also drove for the California Division of Highways. During those years, he leased a cabin from the foreman for the county roads, since he didn't want to live on the ranch.[87]

On January 1, 1934, Jim wrote a letter to his mother in which he said that he was sorry that he couldn't spend the holidays with her, but he and Ralph had gone to McCloud, California, for Christmas on a quick trip, because Ralph had to "be in camp to go to work on Tuesday the 26th."[88] Ralph was fifteen at the time. We don't know if this was a holiday job, or whether Ralph was no longer in school at that time, and we don't know what the "camp" was, although it may have been a Civilian Conservation Corps camp. Also unknown is where Stella was that Christmas. Jim doesn't mention her, so they may have already separated, but that is unclear. Jim started the letter with, "Here it is another year and am wondering what it has in store for us all. I hope that it will be better than 1933."[89] We know that Stella's beloved brother Mat died in October of 1933, so that could be one of the reasons for the comment. Of course, they were also in the middle of the Great Depression, so economics might have played a part as well. Nevertheless, by the end of 1934, Stella had purchased an acre of land in Yreka, California where she would begin to build a house and a new life.

At the age of twenty-three, in January 1941, Ralph enlisted in the United States Army,[90] and with his love of cars, he became a chauffeur in the Second Armored ("Hell on Wheels") Division, stationed at Fort Benning, Georgia. He came home for the Christmas holiday at the end of 1941[91] before being sent overseas. Ralph served in North Africa with the company that routed General Rommel, in the invasion and capture of Sicily, and ended up in the hospital before being sent to England.[92] Ralph took part in the Normandy invasion and fought through France, Belgium, Holland, and into Germany. In May of 1945, Ralph was wounded in action in Germany, after serving three years in Europe. He was awarded six battle stars, the Purple Heart, and numerous other citations earned in the many battles in which he fought. He was honorably discharged with the rank of sergeant in September of 1945.[93]

After the war, Ralph married Janice E. Taylor and they had a son, Stanley, born in Eureka, California, in 1948. Unfortunately, due to Ralph's drinking and physical abuse, the marriage didn't last and Janice divorced him in 1954 or 1955. Ralph was very upset at the loss of his son,[94] and after Stella's death he moved to Klamath Falls, Oregon, where he died on August 19, 1981, aged sixty-three. We know nothing about the remainder of his life.

Stanley lived with his mother in Salyer, California, until he was about ten and then they moved to San Francisco, because Janice wanted him and his half-sister, Kim, to have more choices in life. Janice was from a Native American family and life was hard in the mountain area where they lived. Stan later lived in Lahaina, Hawaii, for about twenty years, where he was a bartender and a sailor. He was referred to as "the mayor," and liked to play basketball and beach volleyball. Stanley was an artistic man who had very discriminating taste. He finally moved to Sausalito, California, where he took up photography in his later years. He developed an aneurism and emphysema, and died of lung failure on March 19, 2011, at age sixty-three.[95]

After Jim and Stella's separation in the mid-1930s, Jim went on to become an even more prominent rancher in the area, and was well known for his barbecuing ability and the special sauce he applied to the meat while cooking. He dug a large pit at his ranch and would cook the meat and deliver it wherever the feed was being held. In 1953, he barbecued for the Fourth of July celebration at Hoopa and served about three hundred.[96]

Some of the newspaper articles that told of Jim's activities are worth mentioning here.

23 May 1941, *Arcata Union*—James Patterson, widely-known Willow Creek rancher and hunter, visited in Arcata Monday. He plans to return this weekend to assist with arrangement for the quarterly meeting of the Northwestern Pacific Railroad surgeons which will be held Saturday night at the Eureka Inn and Sunday at Big Lagoon.

11 Jul 1942, *Blue Lake Advocate*—The James Patterson Circle-P Ranch at Willow Creek was the scene of a Fourth of July barbecue when Jim Patterson entertained a group Saturday. Bear meat with all the trimmings was featured. The bear had been killed last December and held in cold storage since that time...

1 Oct 1948, *Arcata Union*—Party Line by M.P.H. Believe it or Not—"Big" Jim Patterson of Willow Creek dropped in to see us the other day—and our jaw is still ajar with consternation over these quantities...out at the Scotia Labor Day barbecue, Jim cooked 6,700 pounds of meat, served over a ton of potato salad, which required 40 gallons of mayonnaise. No wonder Jim was on his feet from Sunday morning until Monday at 8 p.m. tossing around these pounds and tonnage.

12 Aug 1954, *Blue Lake Advocate*—Barbecue, Dance Set for Willow Creek Project [for emergency center next to Gambi's Resort] .... we drove to the Circe-P ranch to see how Jim Patterson was getting along with the big new ranch house and also what he intended to serve at the Barbecue Saturday evening.

As always, we found the latchstring out and the welcome mat in front of the door. Jim's new home is being built with a U-shape floor plan. One wing, housing the garage, storeroom, pantry, bath, kitchen and dining room, are in use, as is the main hall. A bedroom on the opposite wing is nearing completion, and will be used by Jim for his bedroom, and the ranch office. The view from the main hall and the kitchen is superb, the house being placed on a knoll adjoining Patterson's beautiful little forest park which forms a green background for the building.

Patterson's private barbecue pit is located in the grove near the ranch house and Jim will barbecue the meat and cook the beans for the Saturday barbecue here and take the food to the dinner, which will be served at Gambi's on open-air tables. When we asked Jim if he could provide barbecued meat as tender as last year's barbecue, he assured us it would be just as good. When it comes to barbecuing, we're willing to take Jim's word for it, and as we did not have a knife last year when we ate at the barbecue, it's a cinch that it will be good this Saturday.

Jim had just received a letter from Gordon Manary, superintendent of Pacific Lumber Company at Scotia, telling him that everything would be in readiness for the big barbecue there Labor Day when over five thousand people are expected to partake of the 19 or 20 beeves which Patterson will barbecue. Jim informed us that last year's record of feeding 5,000 people in 35 minutes might be broken this year. The Barbecue King has set his heart on feeding 6,000 in thirty minutes.

Now the real point of all this article is that the Second Annual Emergency Center Barbecue and dance, with ground-breaking ceremonies, will be held at Gambi's Saturday afternoon and evening, and if you desire a fine barbecue dinner, served with Patterson's private-formulae sauce, between 4:40 and 9:30, or enjoy an open-air dance in warm, balmy night air, you're invited to go to Willow Creek, where everything for your comfort is available....

Jim and Stella continued to see each other occasionally throughout the years and never divorced. The exact reasons for their separation are unknown. Jim apparently had a somewhat dual nature, sometimes being very friendly and outgoing, and other times completely ignoring people or being difficult. Stella was said to have spoiled Ralph and that caused some friction between them.[97] Perhaps their lives and interests were just too different to remain together. Stella came back to the Willow Creek area from time to time to visit with Ralph, both before and after the war.[98] One thing is certain, Jim and Stella both continued to live their lives on their own terms. Jim remained on the ranch and Stella went on to Yreka and eventually to Clear Creek, always looking for the next adventure.

Chapter Five

After Stella's Separation from Jim Patterson

Stella's exact whereabouts after she left Jim Patterson are as difficult and mystifying to pin down as the reasons for their separation. However, we have been able to piece together some parts of the puzzle. Some accounts that we have read indicated that Stella had gone back to San Francisco, but we know now that she actually went to Yreka. Sometime in 1934, Stella purchased about an acre of land in Yreka for one hundred dollars. She also borrowed one hundred dollars from the government Housing Act to build a house on the property and had plans to raise rock garden plants to sell.[99] An interesting side note is that the two witnesses to this property sale were Alice Covert, Stella's cousin's wife, and Fred W. Crooks, later to be known as "Dear Sir" in her book *Dear Mad'm.* Stella and Fred had met when he came to work for Jim Patterson a number of years earlier. In April of 1936, Stella wrote a letter to her sister-in-law, Alice Walthall, in which she thanked her for some money that Alice had sent to Stella and described the progress of the house building. She wrote,

> I can't really thank you in terms strong enough. The money that has cleared the land makes life much easier for me.... My little house is coming on nicely, but if you remember when building in Modesto, one has many disappointments over trifles. My little house was to be Spanish in feeling, because I like a balcony where I can sit and gaze at grand old Shasta. Eventually I'll have a tiny patio. This is not

the country for Spanish houses. I thought of a chalet-type house, but I couldn't give up my patio. Here is a crude sketch. House is built on side hill. I do not expect to finish the bedroom this summer. It will have a lovely mt. view and a long low Monterey type porch. The walls (outside) will be aged pine (walnut). The roof—sage green and the trimmings old ivory.[100]

The house was on West Miner Street, about one mile west of downtown Yreka, but unfortunately, it no longer exists. In 1938, Stella bought some adjacent property, increasing the size of her place.[101] Stella is also listed in the Great Register of Voters in Siskiyou County, 1936-1944, in the Greenhorn Precinct. In 1940, Stella sold some or all of her property to Fred Crooks for four hundred dollars. Whether this was the last transaction or not isn't certain, but Stella's will, written shortly before her death, leaves the house and property to Fred.

Sometime before 1942, Stella began to live, at least part-time, at the cabin on the mining claim near Clear Creek. Upon returning to Yreka in November of 1942, she wrote to Winnie Walthall, another cousin's wife,

> I put up a lot of fruit and vegetables down at the claim, also jelly and jams…. You asked in your last letter if I was planning on living at the claim. I should have been glad to do this, but for war conditions. Everyone has practically gone or [is] planning on going and I would have been alone in the community. Since I wrote you last I have been to Arcata again to see the doctor and the dentist. I had a very difficult month. I made this last trip with friends who were going to Arcata. There is a very nice hospital in Arcata and people from Siskiyou make use of it. If ever I need hospitalization I shall go there if possible.[102]

We don't know exactly when Stella began to live full-time on the claim near Clear Creek, but in November of 1944, she wrote to her cousin's son,

> I rarely go to Yreka any more, in fact I have found a little niche here on the Klamath. I bought this bit of property and when the war is over and lumber available I'll build a wee bit

Stella Patterson's Home in Yreka, circa 1940   Lismer Family

Stella Patterson's Cabin on claim at Clear Creek, circa 1940s

Kathi Jones

home for myself and my friends. I hope you'll come to see me and let me meet your bride. I'm sure I'll like her. Never come without letting me know in advance as I am often away…I am busy following my hobby writing. I haven't done any short stories for more than two years, but have worked along leisurely on a full-length novel and am just getting off to an agent in Hollywood and I suppose I'll have to work a lot more on it if it is ever accepted.[103]

As always, she was writing! Letters from 1945 and 1948 indicate that Stella was living at the claim. In 1948, she wrote,

I have lead [*sic*] the life of a recluse for the past five or six years, devoting myself to my writing. For years I practically earned my living with my pen, doing bread and butter stuff, but I finally decided the time had come for me to do something really worth while. Two years ago I completed a major job—a full length period novel—and this year I have done a short tale which is now on the merry-go-round trying to pick off a publisher. The long story has been waiting for revision, which the critic and publisher said must be done. These stories have taken a lot of strength and time but I have been very happy giving my all to the task.[104]

In a follow-up letter Stella wrote,

It is with sincere regret that I must write you I cannot be at the alumnae luncheon June 9. Owing to an injury to my right leg two years ago I find it difficult to travel alone. I have been depending on my cousin, Mr. Edward Walthall, to accompany me, but he is seriously ill and cannot make the trip. I would have to make five changes from this remote part of the mountains where I live. Mail truck, Greyhound bus, Pullman over night, R.R. bus at San Rafael to San Francisco, and lastly another Greyhound to San Mateo where my cousin lives. It sounds formidable and really is quite a jaunt for a much younger woman.[105]

And, just think that some eastern critics of *Dear Mad'm* thought that she was exaggerating about the conditions of the roads! In July of 1948, another letter said,

I would like to see you sometime here at Clear Creek but please write me in advance. This is not my home. I have been here for several years particularly to write without interruption and also because I like the climate and the scenery. It is just an old mining claim which I and several others have been holding for years. When here we live in the miner's [sic] cabins and share miner's fare, but we all like it. It is very much in the rough, but is has a great many attractions for us.[106]

In about 1950, Stella's cousin John Covert and his wife, Alice, came to live full-time on the claim. John was a contractor who had built beautiful wooden bars for some saloons in San Francisco, worked on set design in Southern California, and a bridge and a house for the Hearst family compound in Wyntoon. He was an excellent craftsman and built a large house of stone and wood on the claim between Stella's cabin and Fred Crook's cabin. Alice (Allie) and Stella were very good friends, even though Allie was about twenty years younger. John and Allie's grandchildren spent summers at their home and enjoyed swimming in the river, fishing, playing cards, and listening to Stella's stories. Stella had two dogs, Vicki, the border collie known to all *Dear Mad'm* readers, and another, smaller dog who was very protective of Stella, and would bark and snap at the children if they came too close.

Stella Patterson and Vicki, early 1950s Lismer Family

Stella raised goats and taught her cousin's granddaughter, Claudia, to milk the goats. They went up the hill on a path to get to them. Stella's leg was sometimes swollen, and she used a staff to help her walk. The goats loved her, and so did the children. She was kind, but firm with the children. Stella loved to sit in a chair where she could command a view of the river and the children at play. One time when Claudia's brother Rod was down by the river, he met a bear. They were both scared and ran in opposite directions. When Rod told his mother, she didn't believe him, but Stella had seen it all from her chair and verified his story.[107]

Stella Patterson with Rod, Claudia, and Tom Diridon
From dust jacket of *Dear Mad'm.*

Fred Crooks's ("Dear Sir") cabin was the closest to the river of the three, and it had a bearskin tacked up on the outside. Fred was born in the Dakota Territory in 1885. His family moved to Washington, where Fred lived until he came to California, which was sometime between 1910 and 1930.[108] Fred came to the Clear Creek area in 1933, at age forty-eight. He took out a mining claim and worked the claim for most of the rest of his life.[109] He didn't talk a lot, but he was thoughtful, and when he did speak it was important. He was a hard worker and was honest. Fred treated Stella like a queen and was very protective of her. If the children made too much noise outside when Stella was resting, either Fred or Allie would shoo them further away from her cabin. The children were somewhat intimidated by Fred's gruffness, but he was nice to them and would sometimes walk them to the river, although he didn't like to fish.[110]

Fred Crooks and Vicki, circa 1950   Kathi Jones

Stella's and Dear Sir's beach on the Klamath, circa 1950 Lismer Family

At some point, Stella's health made it impossible to spend all of her time at Clear Creek. In May of 1952, she wrote from Yreka saying that she had been ill for six months and was just getting strong enough to get outside a little.[111] In her last few years, it appears that she spent the summers at Clear Creek and the winters, first in Yreka in her home, and later in Redding at the home of her foster daughter, Thelma Doutt.

Stella moved from her cabin into Fred's during the last few years of her life, which upset Allie greatly. She didn't approve of the move, and it caused a rift in her relationship with Stella that never fully healed.[112] It was undoubtedly easier for Fred to look after Stella there, rather than in her separate cabin. As usual, Stella did what she thought best without concern for what was "proper." How old does one have to be before such "co-habitation" is no longer scandalous? A letter from Stella in June of 1955 gives a good picture of her daily routine while in the mountains.

> I am settled here for the summer and like being outdoors all day. I go with Fred in his jeep up to the Flat where he has his sawmill and lie on a cot (most of the time) in the deep shade of the tall firs and pines. It has been a warm day but not up in the deep woods. We came down to the claims on the river (where my cabin is) about six o'clock and had what I called a patio supper, most everything out of the refrigerator except the strawberries. Fred raises them up at his garden on the Flat, which is high on the mountain-side, and everything tastes so good that is grown at the higher altitude. I have a cot in the woods in a cool shady spot and lie there most of the day. When the shadows begin to lengthen out I do a little work in my flower garden. It has the makings of a charming little rock garden, but I haven't the strength to do much and getting a hired man is a problem.[113]

In another letter, in September of 1955, she says,

> I am writing this in my little cabin in the Siskiyous where I have come to spend the summer and carry on the work I have been doing for the past ten years. I have been greatly interrupted by heart attacks and even now this old heart of

mine is not too good, but the doctors tell me if I rest twenty hours (in relays) I can work four, and so I am writing you about what I have accomplished.[114]

As far as we can tell, Stella did not make her life decisions based on the financial impact they would have. She often didn't have much money and worked as long as she could. Even after she had to stop teaching, at seventy-four, she continued to sell her short stories and grew plants to sell. Stella received a small pension from her years of teaching,[115] but often had trouble making ends meet. Her cousins and her sister-in-law often sent her gifts for her birthdays, at Christmas, and even Easter. She was always appreciative of their thoughtfulness, as these excerpts show.

> A lot of water has run under my bridge since I last wrote you. To say I think of you and Ed many times a day is no exageration [sic]. When I finally got back to town and opened up my little cottage, there I saw evidences of your love and kindness all about me. When I cook a meal I use the nice cooking utensils you gave me. When I get into bed these cold nights I snuggle down under the warm covers you gave me, and here I am sitting in one of your comfortable chairs.[116]

After her birthday in 1954:

> Thank you very sincerely for the check and the dress, which I will write you about when it comes. You are very dear always to remember me on my birthday. Ralph and Jim, a few friends and my dear girl Thelma, always remember me, too. I am here with Thelma as a birthday gift—a gift which includes a home with her for the rest of my life. They have bought a lovely small estate not far from Redding and will build here in the spring. Meantime while work is going on they are living in a big comfortable trailer-house and have bought a small up-to-date trailer-house for me to live in. It is perfectly equipped—like an apartment with tiny kitchenette, bathroom, refrigerator, in fact all of the furnishing needed, and am I a happy woman. I only wish my health was that of a young woman, but I must face the fact that I am 88 and on the twilight stretch of life.[117]

After Easter, 1955:

> I am answering your note & acknowledging check by return
> mail. You are so kind and generous to remember me this
> way. You would have received a letter from me two weeks
> ago, but (and here is a confession which I know you will
> understand) when I sat down to write the letter this thought
> came to me. If I send this letter so close to Easter it may
> look as if I were giving Alice a gentle hint to send me another
> dress or something to wear. You have been so generous that
> I thought maybe you'd overlook this Easter, and that would
> be all right with me. Can you see why I held back? I wanted
> to write you a long loving letter that would not be called out
> just as an expression of gratitude. Do you understand this,
> Alice dear?, for I love you very dearly, like my very own
> sister as you have been these many years, but here again
> you forestalled me, and sent the gift just the same as ever,
> and I am truly grateful.[118]

After her birthday in 1955:

> A birthday wouldn't be a birthday if I didn't hear from you. It
> doesn't need a dress—two dresses—to make me think of
> you as the dearest sister I could have. I wonder if anyone
> of my three sisters had lived if she would have meant to me
> what you have for so many years?[119]

During the last few years of Stella's life, Thelma and her
husband, Everett, looked after Stella during the winter,
when she wasn't on the claim at Clear Creek. In her 1955
Christmas letter, Stella further described her trailer and
her activities.

> As I have written you, I am spending the winter with Thelma
> and Everett and living in a pretty new trailer-house. Thelma
> has a big modern trailer and the one I have is like a tiny apart-
> ment, my living room mostly glass, so I have a nice view of
> the woods and a bit of Mt. Shasta, now entirely covered with
> snow. I have been busy the past month, making sketches in
> watercolors to send away for Christmas. I've made several
> for Thelma and some for my relatives and friends. I am en-
> closing one of a snow mountain (not Shasta), one of many
> we have in this vacinity [sic], Mt. Lassen among them. The

scenery on our Shasta Lake is one of our great attractions. I remember when the little town of Redding was a nightmare of ugly buildings and burnt up landscape. With the coming of the great Shasta dam and lake, all is changed. Green fields everywhere, fine new buildings, lovely modern homes, etc. I think now it is one of the beauty spots of Calif. ...I love it here and am feeling stronger every day.[120]

Although Stella's health was deteriorating in the last few years, her mind was as active as ever. She was full of plans for the publication of *Dear Mad'm* in January of 1956, and the possibility of making it into a movie. She had also written a longer novel which she hoped would be published if *Dear Mad'm* was a success. We get a glimpse of her attitude from her letters, such as this one from October, 1954.

I am not too easy to live with, Alice dear. I have "spells" every now and then and make it very trying for everyone. They think I might die, but I don't. I get up and go on—work in my flower garden, etc, and enjoy life, until, bang, I do it again. Sometime it will be the last "spell" and I will be finding out what the "Great Beyond" has in store for me.[121]

Stella had another "spell" at Christmastime in 1954. After Jim Patterson came to see her she related the following:

He is still working very hard at his stock business, traveling over the mt [*sic*] road early and late. Right now he should retire, but he is threatened with cancer again and wants & needs money to fight for his life. To onlookers he is making money. He has become a very prominent figure in Humboldt—a far cry from the unsophisticated mountain boy I married. He was here to see me yesterday. He has not made money—owing to this cancer, operations, etc., but he keeps out of small debts. I imagine he has loans from the bank.[122]

In January 1955, she wrote,

The beautiful white stole came and was greatly appreciated. You would have heard from me sooner but I spent Christmas week in bed, no Christmas dinner, but I never had a sweeter happier time, lying there with cards and presents & my dear children, Thelma and Ralph, near me. They had a delicious

> dinner which I couldn't eat then, but you know cold turkey is better anyway. I've not been up or out much yet but this p.m. Everett is taking us for a lovely drive in the sunshine. I'm so happily situated here, and Thelma is a devoted nurse. I'm out of the woods now. I'll be getting busy at something very soon. This is a dead secret, Alice dear, about my sickness. I don't write to Daisy or Ed about it. No need to worry them, and I bounce up like a rubber ball.[123]

Apparently the "bounce" didn't last very long. In April she wrote,

> I don't believe in rattling dry bones or post mortems, but just a few words about myself and what happened to me this past winter. On Feb. 3rd I had a pretty bad heart attack. The doctor was called and came for three days, saying he'd have to put me under an oxygen tent in a hospital. Thelma protested that she could take care of me right here, as she had had nurses [sic] training in St. Luke's hospital in S.F. The doctor consented, and to make this story brief, I recovered, and [I am] getting stronger all the time. But I am now a woman with a "weak heart" and have to "slow down, be careful, not overdo" and a lot of other restrictions which if I follow (not too easy for me) will enable me to live and enjoy life for quite a span. As I am rapidly getting into the gay nineties, just another year, why I have everything to be thankful for, and life looks good and I am happy.[124]

During all of these ups and downs in her health, Stella continued to make her plans. While she waited for word about whether her book would be published or not, she wrote:

> I hope to start working on a story that I completed in the rough last year. The book, that had such a good reception with the critics in New York, which I sent off a year ago, is still hanging fire with a publisher. Personally I think they have made too many changes already & have lost what appeal it really had, but maybe something will happen. Some publisher will take it in hand & presto, it will be printed.[125]

We wonder just what changes they made. We know the story is based on Stella's experiences, but, being a storyteller, she used some literary license to combine and rearrange certain events. For instance, although Stella did shoot a cougar, it was not during her years living on the claim, but while she was on the ranch with Jim Patterson. She had gone up to their hunting cabin at Trinity summit, where she encountered the cougar and shot it. Jim wasn't there at the time, but he found the animal dead in the woods nearby.[126] Some other inaccuracies in the book may have been of Stella's doing or perhaps the publisher thought they would make the story better. She was "only" in her late seventies when she began to live at the claim, but eighty is a nice round number and may sound more theatrical, but why change the date of her birthday? It is listed in the book as April 1, whereas it was actually October 14. Also, she moved to Clear Creek from Yreka, not from San Francisco. She hadn't lived in San Francisco since 1905, but it is perhaps more glamorous than Yreka. The story about seeing Queen Victoria in London must be at least somewhat altered, since Stella didn't go to school in England. If she saw the queen, it would have been during her early twenties while on route to or from Paris. These fictional variations may have enhanced the story, but they certainly do not alter the fact that Stella's spirit of adventure never left her, and while the story is not complete non-fiction, it is mostly true.

In July 1955, Stella finally got word that her book had been sold to a publisher in New York. She had originally started sending the book to publishers in 1948, but without luck. She finally changed agents, and the new agent made the sale in a few weeks.[127] Originally scheduled to appear in January 1956, the publication date of the book was postponed until May 1956, because *McCalls* magazine bought the serial rights to *Dear Mad'm* and would publish it in the early spring of 1956. Stella hoped that the serialization of the story in the magazine would create more publicity and therefore more sales for the book. She hoped that publicity in the *Mills Quarterly*, which goes to Mills's alumnae, would also generate interest.[128] She was planning to go to Hollywood and New York to publicize the book on TV and radio, but had some misgivings. She wrote,

By this time you must have my letter telling you about the proposed trip to New York and Hollywood. If I go it will be Hollywood first, & then fly from L.A. to New York. The shorter trip will give me a chance to prove my strength. There are times when I feel equal to it, and then other days, like today, when I wilt at the thought of talking to strangers, making little speeches, and all that goes with this publicity business, but enough of this tonight. I haven't tried on the dresses yet. I just got them out of the P.O. late this p.m. They are both so exactly right for my life in Redding, but I am tempted to send the navy dress back, as (if I go to Hollywood) I shall need something a little more dressy perhaps, and you could exchange, but I'll take a few days to decide this, try on the dress, etc. etc.

Of course, I am too old & scrawny to wear anything low cut & sleeveless. It wouldn't be appropriate anyway. I wouldn't be living up to character, and might disappoint my audience. My book is a personal experience story of an old woman who goes off to live alone in a remote mountain cabin, and what happens to her. She has anything but a lonely life. This is my tale. The title *"Dear Mad'm"* was selected by the Publishers, and they have done some slashing, as well as the agents and critics. I won't know my own child (of my brain), but if it sells, why quibble.[129]

A few days later, she wrote again, discussing her trip and wardrobe.

I am returning the navy blue dress, strange as it may seem. The plaid size 16 is [a] perfect fit. (It opens all way down front). The navy blue is too small, because of the princess or empire cut around waist. My present figure won't take a plain empire or princess cut. I've gained weight around my middle, am rather pudgy, with a good foundation garment I could pull in, but my heart won't stand for that or any controls, so I go without any restraint.

Now I think we can manage the exchange for a navy blue, more dressy affair, maybe in one of these silky looking materials. I'll use this dress for appearances on TV, radio, etc., if I am able to go & fill engagements which is doubtful. The afternoon or dinner dress will come in handy anyway.

I'm going into partnership. Alice dear, I'm asking you to get something more expensive and, therefore am sending $10 which is also one of my birthday presents. This may help pay for the more expensive dress. Everett & Thelma have sent me a beautiful hand bag, & I'll have a new coat, too. All in the natural or camels hair shades. This coat will cover a multitude of ordinary clothes. I'm spending very little money myself—coat, etc., presents. How good everyone is to me.[130]

Alice must have exchanged the dress right away, because two weeks later, Stella wrote again.

The two dresses, navy and purple, were received promptly. I am delighted with both dresses. I had made up my mind to return the purple before I saw it, because I thought you were too generous, but when I donned the purple, I was sold for it. It is more becoming than the navy blue. Purple seems to be my color in my old age. Both dresses are good sizes for me, although I am always short waisted for any style. Both these dresses can be easily changed by a few inches lift in the bodice. I have to do it in all my dresses, a peculiarity of my present figure (which isn't much of a figger [sic] anymore). So, I have two lovely and appropriate dresses, for whatever occasion I may need them. Some days I grow faint hearted over the prospect of appearing on a program and "talking." You know I've always been a talker, and I have laughed at myself for my "tongue tied in the middle & wagging at both ends," but I don't like to be on exhibition. What I do will be to help the sale of my book. I don't have to appear in the public eye before January. Meantime I go down to Redding to be with Thelma, and rest and get used to the idea of "appearances."[131]

The trips were to have taken place in January 1956, and Stella was to have addressed the graduating class of Mills College the following May, but they were not to be. She would not reap any of the benefit of the publication of *Dear Mad'm*, and would never know how her story delighted and inspired so many people. She did at least get to see an advance copy of the book. In her last letter she wrote,

A Merry Christmas to you one and all. May you have loads of happiness in the New Year. I don't know where I stand with news of myself. As you see by date I am at Thelma's, here in Redding, and we are having a terrific storm… I have the first book off the press, just one. It is beautifully done, and illustrated. It looks so good I hope it sells. You'll be getting one as soon as they show up. *McCalls* have [*sic*] sent a photographer out from New York to take pictures of this, or rather my locale for the story, *"Dear Mad'm"* and also of me. This latter I don't like to think of, but I'll have to submit. Grandma Moses does it so nicely, but she's been in training for quite awhile. The story in *McCalls* will appear before the book. I'm still planning on the trip to Mills in May when I'll get a chance to see all of you, and I'll have the two nice dresses to wear at that time. Thank you again for sending them to me. For my pictures for *McCalls*, I'll be wearing the old clothes, shoes, etc., I wore in the story.

Love to you, dear Alice, and all of the family.
Affectionately, Stella

The N.Y. photographer is cooling his heels in Los Angeles while waiting for our storm to wind up its efforts to drown us.[132]

Stella Burfoot Walthall Belcher Patterson died unexpectedly on December 23, 1955 in Redding, California, just three days after writing this letter. She is buried at Lawncrest Memorial Park in Redding, California.

Stella Patterson, early 1950s Karen Tulledo

Stella Patterson's grave in Redding, 2005 Hazel Gendron

Chapter Six

The Aftermath

The storm that Stella referred to in her last letter continued to make life difficult, and the preparations for her funeral were no exception. The weather was miserable, with a great deal of rain and some flooding. Phone service was slow and there were no trains for three days, so even flowers for the service were scarce. The day of the funeral was a raw, cold day. Everett Doutt spent two days trying to get messages through and even started out for Clear Creek to reach Fred Crooks, but fortunately stopped at Dunsmuir on the way, where the Covert family informed him that the message had gone through.

According to her wishes, Stella's funeral was simple and as inexpensive as possible, but even so it cost seven hundred dollars. She had saved $150 in bonds, which left $550 to be paid. Jim Patterson paid two hundred and the rest was paid for by Stella's cousins Ed Walthall, Birdie Boddy, Daisy Willms, and Stella's sister-in-law, Alice Walthall Peck. Her family's love and care was with her to the very end. For the funeral, Thelma dressed Stella in her new, never-worn, purple dress and her white stole, so she went out in style![133]

Fortunately for fans of *Dear Mad'm*, Stella's death did not stop the publication of the book. Correspondence flew back and forth between the publishers, Thelma Doutt, and Evelyn Deane at Mills College. Arrangements were made for publicity in the *Mills Quarterly*, including Stella's obituary, a book review, and the notice about the excerpts to be published in *McCalls* magazine in May. The Mills community embraced

Stella's book, and sales at the campus bookstore and to alumnae were reported to be lively. Also, as stated earlier, President Lynn White used Stella and her book as the subject of his address to the graduating class that year. Notice was also received that a publisher in England had bought the book and that it was being considered for a movie. W. W. Norton and Company, the publishers of *Dear Mad'm*, also expressed interest in Stella's other novel that she had written, but for some reason, it did not get published. Thelma was very pleased by all of the recognition that Stella received, but was grieved that it came too late for Stella's enjoyment.[134]

Copies of *Dear Mad'm* that Stella meant to give as Christmas gifts didn't arrive until the day of her funeral, so none were autographed as she had intended. Thelma found Stella's list of recipients, along with what she intended to write on each one, and she signed them for Stella and made sure they were all sent.[135] By July of 1956, Thelma had collected thirty-three book reports and reviews of *Dear Mad'm* and had received and answered many fan letters.

The year 1956 continued to be a very difficult one. Jim Patterson went to San Francisco in May for a cancer operation, but it was not successful, and he died on September 24, 1956.

Jim's September 27, 1956 obituary from the *Blue Lake Advocate*, summed up his life and reputation:

> **J.B. Patterson, Cattleman and Famed Chef, Dies**
>
> James B. Patterson, owner of the Circle P Ranch at Willow Creek, died Monday afternoon in the Hoopa Hospital at the age of 78 years.... Patterson was in the ranching business for more than 40 years. His first ranch was at Hawkins Bar and 30 years ago he moved to Willow Creek where he raised cattle and opened up and developed the Willow Creek area. He also owned large tracts at Trinity Summit.
>
> At various times he was a packer into the Trinity Alps and gained national prominence for pack trips and barbecues. For 10 years he was the head chef for the Pacific Lumber company's Labor Day barbecue at Scotia. He also used

to prepare a bear meat feed for the Elks club in Eureka and Alameda where he maintained memberships. His skill brought him the title, "Barbecue King."

Patterson is survived by a son, Ralph Patterson of Willow Creek, a daughter, Mrs. Thelma Doutt of Redding, a grandson, Stanley Patterson of San Francisco, four sisters, Celeste Levins of San Rafael, Mrs. Lu Ingersoll and Mrs. Babe Bedashe of Sebastopol, and Mrs. Grace Trobitz of Oakland, and a nephew, Kane Trobitz of Korbel....

Thelma Doutt, wrote the following letter after his death.

Jim passed away Monday. I took him to the General Hospital in Eureka last Monday a week ago and he seemed to get better and the doctor said there wasn't any more they could do for him and since Jim begged to come home the Dr. released him. Sunday Everett came over for the weekend and Jim asked him not to go home. We knew from that that Jim felt bad. That night about 1a.m. Jim started to hemorrhage and we had the Dr. from Hoopa, then at five o'clock we took him down there to the hospital. We are carrying out his wishes and putting him to rest at Willow Creek.

He was conscious right up to the very last and Ralph, Everett & I were with him. He finally just slipt [sic] away. He never regained his strength since the operation in May but we were shocked when the end came so soon.

Ralph and Jim had been estranged for some time, and although Ralph visited Jim when he was sick, they never really made up their differences. In his will, Jim left a thousand dollars to Ralph, a five hundred dollar insurance policy for Stanley, and the rest to Thelma.[136]

Later in the year, Thelma wrote,

We have spent nearly every weekend at the ranch. There were things that just had to be attended to. Jim had sold off acre building sites of late and did not leave it very clear as to whom had paid, and if they had a deed. Some he gave a deed to before the property was paid for etc. However the ranch is clear otherwise and enough money to pay court costs.... I'm going to give Ralph a home site if he wants it, then he'll always have a roof over his head. He's now renting a little shack at Willow Creek and a place of his own would save him some money. He's a very strange fellow and one can't get "close" to him.

The bridge across the river is out but a nice big new one is under construction. Maybe next winter people over there won't have such a hardship. People with school children had to leave their homes and move over to W.C. [Willow Creek] for the winter. We were lucky in having one family close to the ranch that will feed the livestock for us. Guess we should have sold them but the old barn and loading chute was torn down and Jim was too ill to build the new one and to get the cattle out of there over the "emergency road" was quite a chore. Things will just have to stay 'as is' until the ranch is thru probate and until we can get over there in the spring to do them.

This has been the most upsetting year of my life. There are glad and sad memories all intermingled. I still can't realize that Mother and Jim are both gone—and how strange within nine months of each other....[137]

When asked to give information about Stella for the *Mills Quarterly* obituary, Thelma said,

The cover on *Dear Mad'm* gives a brief outline except that she taught school off and on for over twenty years. She craved knowledge, was always studying, reading, teaching and writing on the side. She had a great love for flowers, the great outdoors, animals, and little children, taking me (motherless) at the age of six and being the finest Mother anyone could dream of. Life without her just isn't the same. She never looked, talked or acted old so I never thought of her as nearly ninety. She had so many talents, a fine musician and artist as well as the biggest heart I have ever known. I can't mention one fault in her. If only I could write a book of her whole life as I know it.[138]

If only she had! How much we could have learned from her. Thelma lived to be ninety-seven years old and passed away in Oregon in 2003. We hope that she would approve of our attempt to show the fascinating person that Stella was.

Chapter Seven

Conditions Along the
Klamath in the Early 1900s

In reviewing *Dear Mad'm*, one of the eastern critics commented that the roads couldn't have been as bad as Stella depicted in the book. To that, Thelma wrote, "Everett and I were over this road a couple of months ago and if he [the critic] is like the average Easterner, he would have to be blindfolded to get him across some of the spots...."[139]

These comments, and finding out that Stella's cabin was destroyed in the 1960s when the highway was improved, made us curious about road conditions in the area. When the area was first inhabited there were no roads, just foot trails meandering along the hills and through the forests. These trails were created by the local inhabitants, the Native Americans, fur trappers, a few ranchers, and, after the 1840s, miners. Many trails were established because of the need to get to water and food and were traversed by foot or horse and mules carrying packs. Most trails were not wide enough for wagons yet, so you took as much as you or your pack animal could carry and started walking. It took a long time to walk the trails, for they wound up and down the hills and mountains and in the summer were dry and dusty. In the winter, many trails that followed along the side of the mountains were impassable due to the rains that caused occasional landslides that would block the way. These required someone to clear the trail or make a bypass around the blockage. The first "roads" were wide enough for only one wagon and that made it necessary to move over, as it were, if you should meet an oncoming wagon. This maneuver could be somewhat scary if the road was on the side of the mountain. Bridges were not present then, so if you had to cross a stream or river you did so at a "prescribed place" where it was safe, at fords, not just anywhere. Also, during the winter and spring when the rains were the heaviest, the roads that followed along the rivers might be washed out by a fast-moving, swollen river.

As in Sacramento, gold was discovered in the Siskiyou area in 1849,[140] and the rush to establish claims required the widening of some of the trails into dirt roads to accommodate the wagons that would carry equipment and people to the gold fields. The wider roads were also subject to the climate and became impassable in winter due to deep muddy ruts created by the wagon wheels and washouts that necessitated repairs each summer. The first "roads" were nothing more than cleared dirt paths, but some used a technique called "macadam," which was named for John McAdam, who in the early 1800s on the east coast, improved the road construction system by packing hand-crushed rocks in layers on top of flat ground. Road construction was done by "road gangs," who cut the road out of the terrain by hand and surfaced it. It was a hard, dangerous, and time-consuming task. This type of road worked well for horse-drawn wagons, but when autos arrived on the scene, the roads became inadequate and something had to be done to keep them from deteriorating and becoming unusable. Also, many roads were destroyed by flooding, rain, and landslides so they had to be repaired or rerouted. Overall, traveling in the area at that time was difficult, time consuming, and tiring, to say the least.

On May 7, 1938 an article in the *Blue Lake Advocate*, a newspaper in Blue Lake, California, was entitled, "Trinity area above south fork was wilderness 25 years ago." In this article C.M. Salyer tells of the difficulty of his first trip there in July, 1913.

Cable crossing the Klamath River, between 1938-1943
Happy Camp Chamber of Commerce, Zona Peters' album

Boat transporting a coffin across the Klamath River,
between 1938-1943   Happy Camp Chamber of Commerce, Zona Peters' album

The writer, accompanied by Mrs. Salyer, arrived for the first time in Blue Lake July 23 1913 and spent the night at the Worthington Hotel. We left the next morning at about 4a.m. on a stage bound for Willow Creek. The stage was a light affair drawn by four horses and had none other than Jack Fletcher at the reins. We traveled fast for the time and arrived at the Berry Redwood House for luncheon, changed horses, and resumed our travels, arriving at Willow Creek just at dusk.

Oaks Cafe in Hoopa   Happy Camp Chamber of Commerce, Zona Peters' album

Clear Creek Post Office   Happy Camp Chamber of Commerce, Zona Peters' album

Here we met John Donahue in a light "spring wagon" and traveled over a wagon road famous for its narrow width and steep pitches we finally reached the south fork of the Trinity which we forded and arrived at the Donahue ranch in the early part of the night... we resumed our journey the next morning, our destination being Cedar Creek, a new camp being established by the Corona De Oro Mining company.... Jim Patterson had a contract to cut the lumber for the Cedar Creek flume line. Before leaving we were informed ... that we would have to leave our big trunks ... and pack such necessities as needed in duffle bags for pack train transportation. There we witnessed our first lashing of a pack on a horse and heard the term of diamond hitch, later a familiar term.

The article continues and tells about the wild woods they went through, various ranches they passed, and the homes of well known locals such as Joe Martin, now the home of John Martin otherwise known as Rattle Snake Jake, and Jere Smith of Hawkins Bar, and of crossing the Trinity River at the present site of Salyer over a "tiny wiggly mule bridge" just wide enough and strong enough for one mule at a time. Then they continued their trip over Happy Camp Mountain and through primitive wilderness and down to Cedar Creek to camp.

> And what a camp! We found Jim Patterson and Arthur Clark sitting on a log. There was no sign of a camp.... When evening fell we found there were some 25 of us in "camp" and not a single tent, chair or stove. There were a few pans and pots and supper was cooked on a piece of sheet iron over a fire between four rocks. Here Jim Patterson taught them the "gentle art of making a fir bough mattress." The procedure was for each man to pick his place for his bed and thrash the ground with a pole or long brush. This was to determine whether or not a rattler was in the vicinity. If there was one or more the trashing would cause them to get their gongs going. Finding no rattlers, the bed maker took his axe and cut small fir boughs and placed them criss-cross the shape and size of the mattress desired. This was built up a foot or so in depth and then blankets were spread on it. Comfortable? Well if you are really tired, you'd be surprised.

> Transportation from the junction of the Trinity and south Fork to Helena was by pack train only.

The writer ends his article with the statement that "all present ranches now worthy of the name were carved out under these primitive conditions."

[Authors' note: Charles Marshall Salyer came to the Trinities in 1913 and by 1917 established the town of Salyer.][141]

General road conditions in the Siskiyou area began to evolve in the early 1900s, and when autos and trucks started to use the roads it was determined that just dirt or macadam-surfaced roads were inadequate, so they started to use tarmac, a combination of tar and macadam, which is now known as asphalt. With the advent of logging and logging trucks in the area, another problem arose, that of not enough space on the road for you and the loggers should you meet head-on. The state decided the roads had to be widened, flattened, and made stronger, but it would take many, many years, well into the twentieth century, to develop a road system of wide paved roads and sturdy bridges. In 1917, the first bridge, a wooden and steel cable suspension bridge, was constructed over the Trinity River. In 1936, that bridge was replaced by a metal truss bridge, which also had wood decking.

The Klamath River used to flood often and when it flooded during the 1950s and early 1960s, it took away much of the land where "Dear Sir" and Stella had lived. When the highway was repaired, moved, straightened, and widened, Stella's cabin site was destroyed.

Also in the mid 1960s, the forest service, wanting to reclaim the land, purchased the claims from Stella's cousin, who also had a home on the site, and from "Dear Sir," and they moved their homes to other locations. The river continues to erode and change course and if not controlled could eventually remove all traces of where "Dear Sir" and "Dear Mad'm" once lived.

In general, life for inhabitants in the mountains around Happy Camp and Willow Creek was difficult. They were somewhat isolated from the rest of the state, with poor roads, no power or telephone service, and probably primitive plumbing. They relied on oil lamps and flashlights to see at night, and battery-powered radios to hear world news. There is a beautifully built wooden, battery-powered radio in the Willow Creek Museum as an example of what they used for news in the late 1930s and early 1940s. Only after World War II, with much pressure from the populous, did things begin to change.

River flooding Stella's claim, early 1950s   Lismer Family

Old macadam wagon road leading to Stella's claim   Lismer Family

Landslide road repair near Happy Camp, between 1938-1943
Happy Camp Chamber of Commerce, Zona Peters' album

Road repair near Happy Camp, 1938-1943
Happy Camp Chamber of Commerce, Zona Peters' album

Narrow dirt road near Happy Camp, between 1938-1943
Happy Camp Chamber of Commerce, Zona Peters' album

Road to Happy Camp near Clear Creek
Happy Camp Chamber of Commerce, Zona Peters' Album

Pete Peters with mail truck
Happy Camp Chamber of Commerce, Zona Peters' album

An article from the *Blue Lake Advocate*, August 12, 1954 stated;

> Willow Creek area. Fastest growing area of Humboldt County. In 1940s they first campaigned for power. Then telephone. Last year they developed an Emergency medical center with a doctor's home to attract a Doctor. PG&E delivered power in 1948.

A second article in the same paper stated,

> Before receiving "full" telephone service from AT&T the only phone in Happy Camp in the 1940s was in Brizard's store. A call to Eureka went through Weaverville, Redding, and San Francisco to get there. "One could drive to Eureka and back before the call was complete," said one resident.

Epilogue

A few words about *Dear Mad'm* seem to be in order, since it is the book that sparked all of the interest in Stella Patterson.

The illustrations in the original printing of *Dear Mad'm* were the work of Alice Harvey, one of the first women illustrators and cartoonists to enjoy success. She contributed to *Life* magazine in the 1920s and was a regular contributor to *The New Yorker* magazine between 1925 and 1943. Her illustrations truly captured the spirit of Stella's writing!

For the Naturegraph paperback edition, the cover was done by Vivian Witt, an artist and retiree from Chicago who, with two other friends, was so entranced with *Dear Mad'm* that after visiting with "Dear Sir," they left Chicago and bought Stella's mining claim, living in a house built by Fred Crooks until they died.

The adventures of "Dear Mad'm" have entertained thousands of readers over the years and have sparked many inquiries about the rest of her life. Tourists come to Happy Camp to see the area that they had read about, and the town is happy to have them come. The first "Dear Mad'm" Day picnic was held in August 2011, and the Chamber of Commerce plans to continue to celebrate the spirit of "Dear Mad'm" and "Dear Sir" with an annual event. There is even the possibility of a movie being made of her story, which we hope will happen. Wouldn't she be thrilled to know that her story continues to generate so much interest?

Because of writing this book, we have been given a wonderful opportunity to meet Stella and, through her letters and writings, to understand who she was and what she did. We also gained a better understanding of what life was like then, and an appreciation for all of those strong-minded people who helped develop the mountain communities that we see now. We wonder if we could have survived that experience? Also through Stella, we have met many wonderful people, and for Peter, some wonderful cousins, enriching our lives as well. So, maybe "Dear Mad'm" is still teaching. We hope you have enjoyed her story, learned a little more about who Stella Walthall Patterson was and how she lived. It has been a pleasure for us to write.

Peter Walthall Lismer

Elizabeth Kellam Lismer

San Leandro, California

Endnotes

1. Letter from Ethel Murphy to Sheila Murphy Pickwell, June 15, 1971.

2. Lynn T. White, Jr., President of Mills College, "Words to the Graduating Class," June 10, 1956.

3. Karen Tulledo, telephone interview October 2011.

4. Claudia Diridon Wagner, telephone interview August 31, 2011.

5. Pauline Attebery, interview August 31, 2011.

Chapter One

6. Letter to Alice Walthall, April 16, 1936.

7. George H. Tinkham, *History of Stanislaus County with Biographical Sketches of the leading men and women of the county who have been identified with its growth and development from the early days to the present* (Los Angeles: Historic Record Company, 1921), p. 339.

8. *National Society of the DAR*, Vol. 23, p. 166.

9. Wiliam Lowndes Lipscomb, *A History of Columbus, Mississippi during the 19th Century* (Columbus, MS: S.D. Lee Chapter of the Daughters of the Confederacy, 1909).

10. Eugene R. Walthall.

11. Eugene R. Walthall.

12. Report of Mr. Vallejo, on the Derivation and Definition of the Names of the Several Counties of California (appendix Y), in the Journal of the Senate of the State of California at their First Session Begun and Held at Puebla de San Jose, on the Fifteenth Day of December, 1849. San Jose, CA: J. Winchester, State Printer, 1850, p. 535.

13. George H. Tinkham, *History of San Joaquin County, California: with biographical sketches of leading men and women of the county who have been identified with its growth and development from the early days to the present* (Los Angeles: Historic Record Company, 1923), p. 170.

14. Tinkham, *History of San Joaquin County*, p. 150.

15. Tinkham, *History of San Joaquin County*, p. 151.

16. Tinkham, *History of San Joaquin County*, p. 181.

17. Probate records for Madison Walthall.

18. *A Memorial and Biographical History of the Counties of Merced, Stanislaus, Calaveras, Tuolumne and Mariposa, California* (Chicago: Lewis Publishing Company, 1892).

19. *San Joaquin Valley Biographies,* "Biography of John Madison Walthall," 1905.

20. George H. Tinkham, *History of San Joaquin County, California*, p. 269.

21. Information taken from notes written by Sidney Walthall Lismer about her father.

Chapter Two

22. Stella Walthall Patterson, "A Brief Autobiography," October 31, 1955.

23. Letter from Josephine Brizard Appleton to Elizabeth T. Thompson, April 16, 1945.

24.   Letter from Stella Walthall Patterson to Elizabeth T. Thompson, May 14, 1945.

25.   Letter from Josephine Brizard Appleton to Elizabeth T. Thompson, April 16, 1945

26.   Mills College alumnae file notes.

27.   Mills College and Seminary Catalogue, 1885 and 1886.

28.   Oakland City Directory, 1887-1888.

29.   From the official website for the Eiffel Tower: www. tour-eiffel.fr

30.   Stella Walthall Patterson, "A Brief Autobiography," October 31, 1955.

31.   Description comes from: www.askart.com

32.   Letter from Ethel Murphy to Sheila Murphy Pickwell, June 15, 1971.

33.   San Francisco, California Directory, 1890.

34.   *The Morning Call*, March 26, 1892, p.7.

Chapter Three

35.   *The Bay of San Francisco* (Chicago: Lewis Publishing Co., 1892), Vol. 2, p. 16, and the website for The Belcher Foundation – www.belcherfoundation.org

36.   *The Bay of San Francisco* (Chicago: Lewis Publishing Co., 1892), Vol. 2, p. 16.

37.   *Marysville Daily Appeal*, September 3, 1895.

38.   *Marysville Daily Appeal*, December 1, 1898 and December 7, 1898.

39.   *The Bay of San Francisco* (Chicago: Lewis Publishing Co., 1892), Vol. 2, p. 16.

40.   Probate records for Edward A. Belcher.

41. *The Bay of San Francisco* (Chicago: Lewis Publishing Co., 1892), Vol. 2, p. 16.

42. *Daily Democrat*, Woodland, California, October 26, 1893, p. 1.

43. *The San Francisco Call*, December 10, 1895, p. 5.

44. *National Society of the DAR*, Vol. 23, p. 166.

45. *Arcata Union*, Arcata, California, March 2, 1907.

46. Margaret Wooden. "History of the Patterson ranch on Patterson Road," *Foot Prints in the Sands of Time*, Winter, 2003 and the *Arcata Union*, March 2, 1907.

47. *Arcata Union*, March 2, 1907.

Chapter Four

48. Taken from an article, July 3, 1897, in the compilation "39 Years of Life in Old Denny 1882-1921" – articles compiled by Gay Berrien; index completed by Margaret Wooden.

49. Margaret Wooden, *Footprints in the Sands of Time*.

50. *Arcata Union*, 27 March 1907.

51. *Blue Lake Advocate*, Blue Lake, California, 14 March 1914. From the Susie Baker Fountain papers.

52. *Blue Lake Advocate*, 22 Jan 1927. From the Susie Baker Fountain Papers.

53. *Blue Lake Advocate*, 18 Nov 1922 and 1 Nov 1924. From the Susie Baker Fountain papers.

Note: The Susie Baker Fountain Papers are a compliation of newspaper articles from several different newspapers. They have been indexed and are housed in the Humboldt Room at the library of Humboldt State University. Hereafter we use the abreviation "SBFP" to indicate that an article came from that collection.

54. *Trinity Journal,* Weaverville, California, 6 July and 3 Aug 1918. SBFP.

55. *Trinity Journal,* 30 March 1918. SBFP.

56. *Blue Lake Advocate,* 18 Sep 1909. SBFP.

57. Edward Cooper Waterman interview *Trinity Journal* 13 April 1918. SBFP.

58. *Blue Lake Advocate,* 30 Oct 1915 and *Trinity Journal,* 6 Nov 1915. SBFP.

59. *Blue Lake Advocate,* 5 Jun 1915. SBFP.

60. *Trinity Journal,* 20 Jan 1912. SBFP.

61. *Trinity Journal,* 16 Mar 1918. SBFP.

62. *Trinity Journal* and *Blue Lake Advocate,* 24 Oct 1925. SBFP; Diaries of Mrs. Horel, October 1909; Edward Cooper Waterman interview.

63. *Blue Lake Advocate,* 20 Jan 1923. SBFP, and *Arcata Union,* 18 Jan 1923, from Cindy Trobitz-Thomas.

64. *Blue Lake Advocate,* 20 Nov 1926. SBFP.

65. *Trinity Journal,* 28 February 1925. SBFP.

66. *Trinity Journal,* 17 February 1912. SBFP.

67. Margaret Wooden, *Footprints in the Sands of Time,* Winter 2003.

68. Diaries of Mrs. Lois Horel, Horel Caskey collection, Phillips House Museum, Arcata, California.

69. County School Warrants 1912-1920, Trinity County Board of Education.

70. Letter from Stella to her brother Mat, June 30, 1923.

71. Mills College Alumna file notes of January, 1928 and April, 1930.

72. Letter from Stella to her brother Mat, 9 June 1923.

73. Letter from Stella to her brother Mat, 30 June 1923.

74. *Trinity Journal*, 27 Apr 1918. 19 Jan 1918. SBFP.

75. Lois Horel diaries, 1907, 1909, 1912, 1913, 1915.

76. Lois Horel diaries, 1919; Ruth Horel diary, 1915.

77. *Blue Lake Advocate*, 9 Aug 1930. SBFP.

78. *Trinity Journal*, 15 June 1918, and *Blue Lake Advocate*, 9 Aug 1930. SBFP. Edward Cooper Waterman interview, 30 Oct 2009.

79. *Trinity Journal*, 15 June 1918. SBFP.

80. Letter from Lois Horel to her daughter Ruth, dated October 1, 1917.

81. *Arcata Union*, 9 January 1919. SBFP.

82. Lois Horel diary of 1919; and *Arcata Union*, 10 Oct 1918. SBFP.

83. Edward Cooper Waterman and Cindy Trobitz-Thomas interviews.

84. Note in Stella's Mills College Alumna file, October 1926, says, "SWP and her son are planning to make their home in Modesto, where her brother now lives."

85. *Blue Lake Advocate*, 19 July 1930. SBFP.

86. *Arcata Union*, 7 Aug 1930. SBFP.

87. Edward Cooper Waterman interview, 30 Oct 2009.

88. Letter from Jim Patterson to his mother, January 1, 1934.

89. Letter from Jim Patterson to his mother, January 1, 1934.

90. *Blue Lake Advocate*, 11 Jan 1941. SBFP.

91. *Blue Lake Advocate*, 3 Jan 1942. SBFP.

92. *Arcata Union*, 20 Aug 1943; *Blue Lake Advocate*, 9 Oct 1943; *Blue Lake Advocate*, 14 Jan 1944. SBFP.

93. *Blue Lake Advocate*, 25 Nov 1944; *Arcata Union*, 11 May 1945; *Blue Lake Advocate*, 12 May 1945; *Arcata Union*, 21 Sep 1945; *Blue Lake Advocate*, 29 Sept 1945. SBFP.

94. Letter from Stella to Alice Walthall, June 5, 1955.

95. Kim Kelsey interview, August 29, 2011.

96. Margaret Wooden, *Foot Prints in the Sands of Time*, Winter, 2003.

97. Edward Cooper Waterman interview, October 30, 2009. Letter from Thelma Doutt, July 17, 1956.

98. *Blue Lake Advocate*, 17 Sep 1949 and 6 May 1950. SBFP.

Chapter Five

99. Letter from Roy M. Avery to Edward Walthall, December 5, 1934.

100. Letter to Alice Walthall, April 16, 1936.

101. Public Records from the County Courthouse in Yreka.

102. Letter to Winnie Walthall, Stella's cousin's wife, November 11, 1942.

103. Letter to John Rodney Middleton Covert, November 13, 1944.

104. Letter to Barbara J. Crawford, Mills College Alumnae Secretary, May 23, 1948.

105. Letter to Barbara Crawford, May 31, 1948.

106. Letter to Barbara Crawford, July 7, 1948.

107. Claudia Diridon Wagner interview on August 31, 2011 and talk given by Rod Diridon, Sr. at the Dear

Mad'm Day picnic, Happy Camp, California, August 13, 2011.

108. Census records from 1900, 1910, and 1930.

109. Obituary dated February 25, 1975.

110. Claudia Diridon Wagner interview on August 31, 2011 and talk given by Rod Diridon, Sr. at the Dear Mad'm Day picnic Happy Camp, California, August 13, 2011.

111. Letter to Dear Friends of the Alumnae, May 31, 1952.

112. Information from Rod Diridon, Sr.

113. Letter to Alice Walthall Peck, June 5, 1955.

114. Letter to Evelyn Deane, Executive Secretary to the President of Mills College, September 10, 1955.

115. Letter to Alice Walthall Peck, December 17, 1954.

116. Letter to Winnie Walthall, wife of Stella's cousin Ed Walthall, November 11, 1942.

117. Letter to Alice Peck, October 24, 1954.

118. Letter to Alice Walthall Peck, April 11, 1955.

119. Letter to Alice Walthall Peck, October 13, 1955.

120. Letter to Alice Walthall Peck, December 12, 1954.

121. Letter to Alice Walthall Peck, October 24, 1954.

122. Letter to Alice Walthall Peck, December 17, 1954.

123. Letter to Alice Walthall Peck, January 7, 1955.

124. Letter to Alice Walthall Peck, April 11, 1955.

125. Letter to Alice Walthall Peck, June 5, 1955.

126. Edward Cooper Waterman interview, October 30, 2009.

127. Letter to Alice Walthall Peck, July 15, 1955.

128. Letter to Evelyn Deane, December 1, 1955.

129. Letter to Alice Walthall Peck, October 13, 1955.

130. Letter to Alice Walthall Peck, October 15, 1955.

131. Letter to Alice Walthall Peck, October 31, 1955.

132. Letter to Alice Walthall Peck, December 20, 1955.

Chapter Six

133. Letters from Thelma Doutt to Alice Walthall Peck, January 3, 11, and 31, 1956.

134. Letters from Evelyn Deane, February 14 and June 15, 1956, and from Thelma Doutt, March 26, 1956.

135. Letters from Thelma Doutt to Alice Walthall Peck, September 26, 1956.

136. Probate of will for James B. Patterson, October 30, 1956.

137. Letter from Thelma Doutt to Alice W. Peck, November or December, 1956.

138. Letter from Thelma Doutt to Evelyn Deane, March 26, 1956.

Chapter Seven

139. Letter from Thelma Doutt to Alice Walthall Peck, July 18, 1956.

140. www.siskiyouhistory.org

141. Ben Bennion and Jerry Rohde, et al., *Traveling the Trinity Highway* (Trinity County: Mountain Home Books, 2008), p. 173.

Part Two

A Collection of
Stella's Early Short Stories

Stella Walthall, a Californian by birth, graduate of Mills, studied in Europe, lived in San Francisco, contributed regularly to various periodicals. She wrote under several names: Stella Walthall, Stella Walthall Belcher, Polly Prim, and Mrs. James Patterson. She had stories accepted by *Century Company, Cosmopolitan, Outing, Vogue, Youth's Companion, Argonaut,* and other periodicals. Her "God's Way," (*Colliers*) was one of the stories accepted in the Collier short story contest. On the following pages are eight of her short stories.

The Stage Driver

Stella Walthall Belcher

May 18, 1895 – Denton Journal, Denton, Maryland (listed as originally from the Argonaut)

We had ridden three hours with a stupid stage driver, and I was chagrined and disappointed. I had engaged the front seat two weeks in advance and had expected to have a chance to study one of the old time stage drives on his native heath; but, though it was said he had been on the route 20 years, he chewed a quid of tobacco and could not be induced to talk. An occasional grunt of assent or dissent was the most he vouchsafed us, and it was with a feeling of relief we changed stages at Murphy's and had another driver.

The drive from Murphy's to Angel's is over 15 miles of dusty, uninteresting road, and we had not looked forward to the prospect with pleasure, but our new driver had an air of business and a looseness of tongue that were very refreshing after the mummified silence of the other man and promised well for our entertainment.

Then, too, we saw we had made a mistake about our first driver. The second man was of course the old stager, with his many thrilling adventures and hairbreadth escapes, while the first man was evidently a novice in the business. We took our seats and prepared ourselves for a most interesting time.

"Hope you're all comfortable, ladies," began our second man in a manner very different from the other gruff bore. "I do like mighty well to have ladies in the front seat with me, but I'm quite a fav'rite with the ladies, it seems—they always want the front seat."

"Oh, I see you are the old stage driver," I exclaimed, "and you will tell us some of your interesting stories. How lovely! What is your name?"

"My real name's—no matter. But they call me Tennessee up here. You see, I come from Tennessee, an' I've got the southern twang, and when I first come I talked a heap 'bout my native state, an' I bragged some, too, I guess, coming from the south, you know, and the boys like to josh a fellow. But I've traveled round so much that I've lost most of my twang—knocked 'bout considerable in my day. Fellow can't help rubbing on some polish, you know—I expect that's why I'm such a fav'rite with the ladies. It's real funny how all the old maids get stuck on me and the widders, too," Tennessee chuckled. "By jiminy crickets! Excuse me if I got off a swear word now an then—I don't know which is the worst, old maids or widders." I took a sly glance at my companion, who was a young and pretty widow who lived in San Francisco. "I'm writing a book on my experience with the women."

"Why," said the widow, "I should think you would get married with so many to choose from."

"Well, it does seem that way. You see, I did try it onct. I'm a widderer—got sons over 20 years old. Wouldn't believe it now, would you? Most people take me to be 'bout 30. I'm by rights over 40; but, great Jupiter whipstitch!—excuse me, we old stagers can't help a little profanity—I wouldn't have any trouble marrying. I most always propose to the women before I get them through." My pretty companion looked alarmed. "The women like it, particular the widders. Now we're coming to a little down grade. Got on a pretty heavy load, so guess we'll take it easy. Go 'long there, Suse—Nick, you old rack o'bones."

We rounded the brow of the hill, and the horses began the steep descent with a gentle trot, but within a few seconds their speed had accelerated to a hard gallop. The old Concord coach rolled from side to side, and we seemed in danger of upsetting, but our time had not yet come, and we reached the level road in safety. The widow and I were gazing at Tennessee with admiration. How fearless he was! What splendid driving! But a timid man on the back seat was first to recover his speech.

"I think you had better use your brake, driver," he said in a querulous voice. "That driving was altogether too fast for a heavy coach."

"Listen to that old duffer," said Tennessee, sotto voce. "Guess he never seen a hill before." Then he raised his voice. "Well, I did try," he said, calmly glancing back. "Why, Lord, the brake's gone!" he exclaimed.

We all looked at the rear wheels in dismay. The brake was gone in truth.

"Well, we'll have to go back; that's plain," said the timid man.

"What! Pull up that hill?" said Tennessee, with disgust. "Not if I know myself. We'll be all right. I never had an accident in my life. Why, last week I had 12 people on board—two women an a kid here in front—an one of the front wheels rolled off right on this down grade an rolled 100 yards down the road, an we just settled down kind of comfortable like an I never spilled a person or broke a screw. Oh, I'll get you through safe, you can rest easy on that."

We were trotting along at a lively rate, and I glanced nervously at the heavy axles. I hoped devoutly that the wheels were secure.

Tennessee continued his talk with the most nonchalant air, as if brakes and wheels and things of that kind were of minor consideration. "This house we are coming to is the only postoffice between Murphy's an Angel's" he said. "Nice little woman keeps it—might sweet on me—plucky, too, I can tell you."

We drew up at the door, and a kindly faced woman came out with the mailbag. She gave us a little nod of greeting and retreated modestly into the doorway. Two or three towheaded children peered out from behind her skirts at the stage people.

"The schoolma'm's going down this morning," said the post-mistress.

"We're pretty well loaded," said Tennessee. I thought so, too, and wondered where we would put the schoolmistress, but Tennessee seemed equal to any emergency. He started the horses.

"Good morning to you, ma'am," he called to the woman and wafted a kiss from the tips of his fingers, presumably to the children, but I thought with intention to show us how he managed those things with the ladies. A few rods beyond we stopped, and a sunburned girl came out.

"Good morning," she called in a fresh, clear voice. "Have you room for me?"

"Oh, yes," answered the obliging Tennessee. "Always room for one more. Got any trunks?"

"Yes, two," and she glanced apologetically at two enormous saratogas which stood just by the door. We wondered where they would be put, but Tennessee never hesitated. The trunks were placed somewhere on the back, and our driver sprang nimbly into his seat again. We started off on a brisk trot, and Tennessee launched forth in a string of thrilling narrative.

"See that hole over there?" he said. "A friend of mine dug out $3,000 in one day there. He wants to sell the mine now. I'm the agent. I tell you that I get more of that sort of thing than I can attend to. Why, I make more than four times my wages just selling out claims. Don't want to buy a claim now, do you? No? Well, here's something more interesting than claims—for a paying business beats claims all hollow—that's stage robbing. See that tree over yonder? That's where I was held up last time. Robber didn't get anything, though. That's onct when he miscalculated."

I looked about quickly. We were now in a dusty wilderness of pine and chaparral. Not a sign of human habitation near. Tennessee saw my nervous glance.

"Mighty lonesome looking now, ain't it? See them bullet holes in my stage cover? Them was put in when we were attacked by six robbers over here by Joaquin Murietta's old home."

I felt my blood run cold. I had not seen the bullet holes before. The timid man gave vent to an audible "Ah!" and the others preserved an awe struck silence.

"Why," continued Tennessee, "I guess every stone and tree had hid its robber some time or other 'long here. I've had 15 or 20 holdups, an that's nothing compared to some of the old timers."

"Do you think there is any danger at this particular time?" inquired the timid man.

"Why, that's hard to tell," said Tennessee dubiously. "It was just here where we had that last holdup two months ago, an one of the passengers and two of the robbers was killed. The papers never got the straight of that. You see, it was that holdup which showed me that the little widder postmistress was stuck on me. I was coming along here that day—had on a Wells-Fargo shotgun messenger an a lot of passengers. There was about $100,000 in bullion under the seat, an the messenger held a loaded gun in his hand all the time. When we got just 'bout here, coming up the hill, I saw the bushes move right there, an I said, kinder under my breath, 'Robbers!' I whipped out my pistol, an the messenger aimed his gun; but, Lordy, who do you think it was? Why, the little postmistress back there. We came nigh shooting her. She looked frightened nigh to death an was white as a ghost.

" 'Don't shoot,' she said, kinder soft like. 'Four men are going to rob the stage. I heard them planning it. They want to stop you before you git to the top of the grade, but if you hurry you'll git there first an maybe can git away on the down grade. Goodby, an be quick,' an she got out of sight in a twinkling. Done that for me, you see. We never waited to thank her. That's one thing I object to in these here mountains—you've got to sacrifice politeness sometimes.

"Well, I just gave my horses a cut, an they jumped forward. That plucky little woman got out of sight pretty durned quick—had a horse, I guess. Well, we got to the top of the hill first, an, by Jupiter snupgrass—excuse me, always use strong language when I git excited—right on the other side was four masked men a-coming it up the hill as hard as they could tear."

There was a breathless silence on the stagecoach. The horses were pulling up that very hill, and there was a possibility that we would be held up too. Tennessee was getting a quid of tobacco. He kept us hanging breathless on his words until he had the morsel well rolled into his cheek.

"The first glimpse they caught of us they jumped behind trees an called, 'Halt!' but we were on the brow of the hill, an I was prepared. I'd fastened the reins round my waist an guided with one hand, while I used the other for my six shooter. The messenger shouted, 'Let her go!' It was just here, ladies. We left two men stretched out. I killed two robbers an wounded another. The shooting scared the horses, or I think I'd have finished all four. That durned messenger—excuse me—was so scared that he shot one of my horses. Not used to the biz you see. Of course the horses stampeded—it's bad enough to hear the firing without being peppered by an unresponsible man who is frightened into next week.

"Well, they started on the dead run down the grade, an I had to drop my pistol an hang on to the lines. I tell you we buzzed round them turns—sometimes two wheels standing off the grade to onct. When we reached the bottom of the hill down at the station, the old hoss dropped dead, an the people on the stage just come up to me a crying an a-thanking me for saving their lives an took on turrible. Look—at that rock!" he ejaculated. We gazed with startled eyes in the direction he had indicated. "Oh, I guess it's all right this time, but I always expect to have a man step out from behind that rock—finest place to rob a stage in the country. Two men held me up there about 15 years ago, when I first began to drive here. Didn't get anything, though. Now we're past. Guess that's a sigh of relief, ain't it? This is a mighty dangerous country 'bout here, but I guess I'll git you through, ladies. Don't you fear. If we git attackted, just sit still—keep perfectly cool an calm, an you probably won't git more than two or three scattering shots."

We were all well frightened by this time. The little schoolmistress on the back seat held her peace, but the rest of us were looking about nervously and trusting our lives to this wonderful Tennessee. The pretty widow was no longer haughty and distant, but at every noise in the brush grasped the arm of the brawny driver and looked appealingly into his face.

"Now, ladies, when we start down this mountain, we are on the home stretch to Angel's. Just one mile more. I always feel glad when we pass this knoll. Joaquin Murietta held me up right here the first month I was on the road. I had five miners on board, an they showed fight, an they got the worst of it too. I just held my horses an kept cool. Indiscretion is no kind of valor, you know. Well, Murietta strung up every one of them five miners to a tree an told me to go into Angel's an say that Tennessee was the only man about with any sense, an for other people to take warning. That's the old tree over there, an there's the ropes yet. See them right there."

"Oh, do drive on fast, do drive on!" we all exclaimed shudderingly.

"Well, I guess we'll have to go on, an pretty fast too. The horses can't hold back much on this down grade. If we turn over, ladies, I guess it will be on my side, so just be prepared to swing yourselves out."

Down we started. In a few seconds the horses were galloping, and in a few seconds more they were running. Five badly frightened people hung on in desperation to the seats, and the pretty widow hung to the arm of Tennessee. His feet were braced against the dashboard, and his body was stiffened out as he hung on to the taut lines. Swinging, bumping, pitching, we careened down the long hill and went tearing into the little mining camp of Angel's.

We drew up with a flourish at the door of the primitive hotel and fairly fell into the arms of Tennessee, who had sprung to the ground to receive us.

Six thankful, admiring people stood in the tiny hotel parlor awaiting the next stage and driver. The little brown schoolmistress was there too.

"Why," said the little widow, "I think I should have died of fright on that dreadful road if it hadn't been for Tennessee."

"Yes, indeed," cried No. 2. "The very thought of that brave man kept me calm, and I know if any one else had been driving we would have been killed surely. What a splendid fellow he is!"

"Just the kind of a driver I have always heard about," cried No. 3.

"You could pick him out from a thousand as a regular old stager," said No. 4.

"He's the bravest man I've ever seen," said No. 5.

"He's a great, big hearted, fine fellow," said the timid man, "and a genuine hero too. I'm thankful we had such a competent man over that fearful road."

"Pardon me," said the little brown schoolmistress, who had been a silent listener, "but I think you are all mistaken. Tennessee isn't much of a hero. He's only been in the state two weeks, and to judge by his driving he never saw a stage before, and—well, the postmistress is engaged to the shotgun messenger, and all those robbery stories he told you happened to Fred Green, who drove you down to Murphy's this morning. Evidently Tennessee thought something was expected of him and proved himself equal to the occasion."

Trial by Fire

Stella Walthall Belcher

*Published in the San Francisco Argonaut
(exact date unknown) Reprinted in the
Mountain Democrat, Placerville, CA March 7, 1896*

The major was one of the many well born Englishmen who came to California with a younger son's portion and a small monthly allowance and hope to make a fortune on a vineyard or a wheat ranch. The plan always looks feasible in England, and the agent assures his victim that the thousand pounds will buy a ten acre plot, plant vines, build a decent bungalow and tide the owner over until the vines shall bear and bring him a harvest of good American gold.

The major was going the way of many of his English friends. The £1,000 legacy was gone, and the monthly allowance of £20 (which, viewed from a distance, seemed large) always grew painfully small as it neared California and the debts it was supposed to cover. The major's little mountain vineyard had been destroyed by phylloxera, and he was living on the uncertain promise of a number of green shoots, called, respectfully, "the olive orchard." But the major was not unhappy. When he was not tilling the soil, he sat on his little veranda, with his brier wood pipe between his teeth and studied the long, narrow, picturesque Napa valley far below.

It may be that the major's failure to succeed in the grape business was not the fault of the country, but that his genial, unpractical nature was the true obstacle to success. The major was, in fact, the most helpless Englishman who ever came to California to take care of himself. The poor fellow became so convinced of this after a short trial that he engaged a man to set as valet to himself and incidentally cook the meals for both.

The major was a solitary bachelor then. The gods alone know in what unpropitious moment he picked up Pete to hang about his neck, a millstone of inefficiency. Pete's poverty must have been his recommendation and the major's poverty the excuse for keeping him. Pete had about as much knowledge of laying out and caring for a man's wardrobe as the major had of running a ranch. The consequence was that the major often presented himself at his friends' houses in the most surprising garb—a combination of white duck trousers, black frock coat, and russet hunting boots being one of Pete's masterpieces. In his capacity as cook Pete was not one whit more efficient and often suffered mental agony over the ponderous directions of the major's French cookbook, which were like the hieroglyphics of the ancients to his clouded intellect. Considering the diet of sour bread and tinned meats which Pete provided, it is only less than marvelous that his benefactor was still alive.

When the major married Ellie Smith, a pretty San Francisco girl, Pete was promoted to be manager of the ranch and expended his grooming talents on the pet mule. The major's wife was "artistic." She had studied sketching and did some really clever bits. Her admiring husband was sure that she possessed the divine afflatus, and consequently much time was devoted to art and little time to ranching.

But this was not without protest from one individual. Not that he was disturbed by lack of work, but poor Pete was oftener than not the unwilling model for Ellie's clever studies. One day Pete posed for "the Man with the Hoe." His temper was particularly tried on that occasion, for he had taken up his tool with the honest intention of weeding the primitive vegetable garden. Though he had scudded through the back yard and climbed the rear fence he had not counted on meeting his young mistress in the barnyard. He began to wrestle with the weeds and pretended not to see her. His education, however, had not included a sight of Millet's picture, or he would have fled down the mountain side in utter despair.

"Stop, stop, Peter, right there. Don't move an inch," called the sweet voice that drove him to madness. "Kenneth," Ellie called to her husband, "look. Isn't it wonderful? The lights, the pose, the very landscape like"—

"'The Man With the Hoe,'" shouted the major gleefully. "I'll get your paints, Ellie. Hold on, Pete!" And before that honest son of toil had time to collect his scattered senses, he found himself posing in a very uncomfortable attitude, with the Napa valley lying at his feet and the major's familiar phrases ringing in his ears—"fine pose—jolly good subject—delicious coloring."

After Pete had posed for a hundred or more indifferent works of art without names, he began to think of deserting his master and leaving him to a just and awful fate. But this stupendous blow was averted by the arrival of Brompton Edwards, another Englishman, who had come to learn practical ranching under the direction of his father's old friend, the major.

After a week had been given up to driving his protégé about the valley and introducing him to the English colony, the major returned to his daily routine of pruning olive trees and digging out worm eaten grapevines. Ellie soon discovered in the young man's clean cut features and fine, athletic figure an entirely new field for art study, and Edwards found the time pass more pleasantly as a model than as an embryo rancher. They were together during most of the daylight hours. When Brompton was not posing for a wild Norseman or a Greek hero, he was sitting very close to Ellie, criticizing, in soft, caressing tones, the sketches of himself which she had been doing. Without actually straying from the path of duty, Ellie was treading on dangerously uncertain territory. She quite frankly admitted to herself that she was pretty and charming, and being of that mind, she did not repress comparisons between her husband and the younger man.

Matters had arrived at a state where a warm hearted but vain young woman needed a friend with the strength to hold up a good, powerful, unrelenting mirror for her to gaze into. Pete could have held up the mirror with right good will, but he did not know how. In those days he followed the major around with doglike devotion and only glowered when Ellie came out to the orchard one morning with her paints and succeeded in bringing upon herself a scolding from her overindulgent husband. She held her head very high and stiff, and marched over the hill some distance away, where she seated herself and pretended to sketch, but was in reality nursing her injured feelings to keep them alive. The major watched her disappear with a pained expression on his good natured face, and then went dejectedly into the house. Pete was deeply incensed against Ellie, and made another solemn vow to desert the ranch. It was the ninety and ninth time that he had done so, and this time he sealed the vow with an oath.

The long grass on the Napa hills was burned and crisp and Ellie was daubing yellow ocher and burnt umber over her canvas with vicious strokes. She was not giving any attention to her work, however, for an athletic form stood between her and the landscape, and she was indulging in a very foolish day dream. To do the little woman justice, she was not in love with Brompton, but her vanity had been stimulated to such wonderful activity by his youthful gallantries that she fancied he was deeply infatuated with her. She wondered if he would ever tell her that he loved her. If she could only have some test of his love, what a satisfaction it would be!

Over on the mountain side a half mile away Pete leaned on his hoe and watched a thread of fire crawling like a red snake through the underbrush of chaparral and manzanita. He knew only too well that no human power could stop it, and that within a few minutes the gentle breeze would cause a flying spark to fall upon the long dry grass, and puff—the crawling snake would become a great swirling, galloping mass of flame and smoke and would pass over the very place where Ellie sat sulking and dreaming. Pete had firmly determined to leave the ranch. He had washed his hands of these people. He would not—but the grass was on fire, and Pete made a dash for the house, yelling at the top of his lungs for the major.

The volume of smoke was rising high when Ellie rose to her feet and sniffed the air. Before she could gather up her paints a thin rim of fire ran along the top of the little hill above her. The small birds and insects rose from the ground with a whir and scattered down the hillside. Ellie glanced quickly backward and saw the fire licking up the grass as it bore down upon her and the smoke rolling heavenward in dense, sooty clouds. She did not lose her presence of mind, but remembered a small plowed field a short distance away, where the flames could not reach her, and ran nimbly down the hill, with her fluttering skirts gathering cockle burs and sticker weed as she sped.

When she was fairly on the plowed ground and gasping for breath, she saw the young Englishman tearing along the hill at a frantic rate. Through the smoke he looked pale and frightened. Ellie felt a thrill of satisfaction. Here was the longed for proof of his love. He thought she was in danger and had come to her rescue. A deep blush mounted to her cheeks and her heart beat to suffocation. But he did not seem to see her. It was evident to her that he was crazed with fear and would plunge into the fire in search of her. Merciful God! He would be burned.

"Brompton!" she screamed. "Dear Brompton, I am here— safe."

The fire was very close, and she had to throw herself flat on the ground to escape being burned. She gave one more despairing cry as she felt the hot breath scorch her clothing. "Brompton! Brompton! Brompton!"

A great wave of smoke and flame swept around the edges of the plowed ground, and for a minute nothing could be seen or heard. Fortunately for Ellie the dry grass burned like tinder, and the fire was soon roaring down the hill toward the valley.

When Ellie, choked and frightened, lifted her head, she saw the thin, long, scantily clad legs of her husband bounding over the blackened earth toward her. His duck trousers were smeared with soot, and he had a wet blanket about his shoulders. He could not speak, but caught Ellie in his arms and burst into stifled sobs.

Back of them was heard the voice of Brompton Edwards. "Hello there, major!" he called. "I had a very narrow squeak of it. My hammock and books are burned to tinder by this. By Jove, old fellow, you are burned yourself, aren't you? Your wife was safe enough. I knew she could take care of herself."

But Ellie buried her head in the wet blanket with a shudder and burst into tears of shame and contrition.

"Well, well," gasped Pete, who had stumbled up the hill with a bundle of wet sacks. "I never was so plaguey scared in my life. Thought you'd be burned sure, Miss Ellie. Me and the major'll have a fine time next week clearing"—

For Pete had reconsidered his ninety and ninth vow. Indeed it was only a week later when he was speculating if there was ever a happier couple than the major and his Ellie. And Pete beamed as he thought of the ignoble part Brompton Edwards played on the day of the fire.

A Fatal Climax

Stella Walthall Belcher

The Century Magazine, Vol. 53 Issue 1, Nov. 1896

Jim Rodes, better known as "Spooky" Rodes, was one of the left-overs after the first mining-fever subsided in California. He lived for over twenty years in Tuolumne County, and though he never rose above the station of hanger-on in a mining-camp, he attained a local fame unique and unenvied.

Rodes had no particular place of habitation. He was like a bird of passage, flitting from place to place, and taking philosophically such fare as fell in his way. He owned a decrepit nag, which served to carry him over the rough country roads, for Jim had no intention of subjecting his shoes to unnecessary wear and tear.

The old man passed his winters down in the foot-hill country, and in the spring made a yearly visit to the mountains, where he remained until the snow and frost drove him back to a more congenial clime.

"Spooky" began his yearly visits at the house of one Andy Simons. He tied his horse under the giant oak which the thrifty Simons used for barn and stable, and took up his abode in the three-roomed house. There was already a large family, but that did not discourage Jim. There was always plenty of bacon and potatoes at Andy's, and a full stomach was more to Jim than a palace. He would prolong his visit one, two, three weeks, as long as the hostess would tolerate him; and finally, when his welcome was worn threadbare, and even the baby began to offer infantile snubs, Jim saddled his horse and moved along.

"Spooky" Rodes was a generous soul. He presented Mrs. Simons with a fine new butter-mold upon his arrival, and now that he intended visiting the Twillers, the nearest neighbors, he saw no harm in quietly pocketing the half-dozen plated spoons, the pride of Mrs. Simon's heart, and carrying them as an offering to the Lares and Penates in the Twiller household.

Thus Jim moved about the circle of his acquaintances, and in moving carried with him many little articles of value or virtu. Indeed, the good people of Tuolumne had come to know so well Jim's give-and-take code of etiquette that on his arrival spoons were consigned to the bottom of the flour-barrel, new linen was stowed away on the rafters, and a general counting up took place at night. But even with this vigilance, Jim managed to make offerings to his various hostesses ranging in value from soft-soap to plated ware.

Jim had some thrilling experiences—at least, he could tell about them in a way to thrill his audiences. They would sit listening with open mouths and straining ears until Jim had reached his climax; then, drawing long breaths of relief, they would sink back into their chairs, as he led them gently down by easy steps to a place where he could satisfactorily conclude his story.

But Jim's high sense of the fitness of things once led him into a grievous snare which obliged him to choose between himself and an artistic climax. Like a true raconteur, he sacrificed himself, but brought down upon his head the derision of a younger and more irreverent generation, by whom he was ever after known as "Spooky" Rodes.

Jim was making his annual visit at the Twillers'. Supper was over, and the men were tilted back against the house with pipes and tobacco, while the women-folk "rid" the table and pared the potatoes for breakfast.

"I reckon," said Jim, meditatively, "thet none o' ye hev hearn tell on thet experunce I hed with the Injuns. I reckon it war nigh on thirty year ago, when I war crossin' the plains, thet the experunce thet I'm 'bout to tell ye happened. I war ridin' a fiery black hoss, an' I got clear ahead o' the train,—more'n ten mile ahead, I reckon,—when all to onct I heerd behind me the dernedest yell. I jerked a look backwards, an' seen a band o' thirty or forty Injuns a-comin' it towards me, with their bows all a-aimin', an' their toes dug into their hosses' flanks; an' sez I, 'It's all up with ye, Jim Rodes.' But I reckoned it'd pay to sell my life dear, so I clapped my spurs into my hoss's flanks, an' 'way we went.

"Right afore us war one o' them tremenjous big cañons ye've hearn tell on back on the plains—the Grand Cañon, or the royal George, or somethin' like thet. Well, I didn't see much diff'runce, so I put my hoss right for the cañon, an' pell-mell up we went—the cañon gittin' narrower an' narrower every minute, an' the walls on the sides just risin', I reckon, nigh about a thousand feet. Anyways, no sun ever got down to the bottom, an' 't war gloomy as the grave, an' them Injun devils whoopin' it up behind. On they came, boys. I could hear their hosses snortin', an' the arrows whizzed by my ears like a swarm o' bees. Off went my hat, my coat-sleeves were ripped open, old hoss's ears bleedin' with the arrows, an' the walls gittin' closer an' closer together, an' it gittin' powerful dark too; an' then we dashed past a big rock, an' oh, Lordy! There I saw a sight to make my hair stand on end an' the cold sweat to run offen me; an' oh, Lordy! There, right in front o' me, about twenty yards ahead, the walls come together, all but jest wide enough for a waterfall a thousand feet high to come tumbling down; an' oh, Lordy!—"

"Great Scott!" cried an anxious listener, "what did you do?"

"Why, oh, Lordy! Them Injuns come tearin' on behind, an' I jest plowed my spurs into the old hoss, an' on, an' on, an' on—"

"What about that waterfall?" cried the youngest Twiller boy.

"What in thunder did the Injuns do to ye?" cried Twiller.

"Why—why—the waterfall—an'—an' the Injuns," stammered Jim—"why, dernital, they killed me!"

NOTE: This story is included in the Cornell University Library Making of America Collection, which is a digital library of primary sources in American social history from the antebellum period through reconstruction.

Chiquitito

Stella Walthall Belcher
Illustrated by Henry S. Watson

*St. Nicholas: an Illustrated Magazine for Young Folks. Vol. XXVI,
Part II, May – Oct. 1899, p. 1026. (The Century Co., New York)*

Little José was a small, starved specimen of "swiperino" (the name the American soldier has facetiously given his Cuban brother), and if it had not been for a kind-hearted American officer the little fellow would now be buried in the trenches covered with a foot or two of earth, and no one would have known how much gratitude one small Cuban could possess.

It happened while the invading army lay outside the city of Santiago. The base of supplies was twenty miles away, and every piece of hardtack and bacon had to be brought in on mule-back over a trail a foot deep in mire and liquid vegetation.

There were thousands of refugees from the city and thousands of soldiers to be fed, and the commanding general sent word that all the Cubans and foreigners who were able must come four miles farther down the trail to make easier the distribution of provisions. Soon a famine-stricken procession was plowing painfully through the mire: mothers hugging to them half-starved babies; fathers and husbands dragging along their feeble women folk; children struggling to keep near their parents—all a sad, pitiful spectacle, which wring the hearts of the kind Americans.

Little José clung to his mother's skirts, and looked bravely up into her pale, worn face. It was a desperate struggle for him to keep along, and he tripped, picked himself up, tripped a second time, and then, being too weak to try again, the crowd pushed him aside, and the little fellow sank in the mud. The mother gave one backward look, like a dumb animal in pain, and struggled on to save herself and her babe; and that would have been the last of José had not an American officer gathered him up and carried him to his tent.

It was impossible to tell what José looked like, for he was covered with a shell of Cuban mud. The officer stripped him, tucked him in a blanket, and gave his clothes to an old camp-follower to wash.

The youngster was literally stuffed with bacon and beans and hardtack by his benefactor, and a few hours later was strutting about the camp, clean, well fed, and fairly bursting with happiness.

Three days went by. José had begun to struggle with the English language. He could say, "Ee t'ank yo'," and "Yo no sabe de Englis'," and some other incomprehensible lingo. He ran errands; he ate ravenously; he slept in his benefactor's tent'; he was the kind officer's devoted shadow; and all this while the Americans waited outside the gates of Santiago.

Then, one day, the Stars and Stripes floated over the city, and the officer saw that it was necessary to part with the little refugee and send him home to his friends. Therefore, loading a sack with rations, and mounting it and the boy on a decrepit mule, he bade them God-speed, and started them in the direction of Santiago.

"Ee t'ank yo', Señor Offeecer, ee t'ank yo'!" cried the boy, with tears in his eyes.

And the officer said:

"Adios, adios, querido muchacho" ("farewell, farewell, dear child")' and to his friends: "That is the last I shall hear of my refugee."

But he was mistaken. Cubans have gratitude.

Two days later José appeared in camp. His face was stretched in a broad smile, and under him arm he carried tenderly a poor starved chicken, which had barely enough animation to stand up.

"'HE 'S FO' YO',' HE SAID SIMPLY, AND TURNED TO GO."

His owner placed him on the ground before his friend the officer, and proudly smoothed down his very ragged feathers. Then, stepping back from his pet, he spread out his little brown hands.

"He's fo' yo'," he said simply, and turned to go.

The officer caught the boy by the shoulder, and turned him right about.

"See here, my little man," he said kindly, "I'm much obliged. But you need your chicken more than I do. Take him home."

José shook his head.

"Yo no spick de Englis'. Yo no sabe." He pointed to the chicken. "He name –'Chiquitito.' He ees fo' yo'. Ee t'ank yo'."

That settled the matter. José remained firm. This chicken was his all, and he gave it to his friend, the Americano.

A string was tied about the chicken's leg, and he was anchored to the tent-pole, where he attracted much questionable attention from all the hungry soldiers. They looked him over with longing eyes, and sized up his points at mess-times, wondering whether he'd taste better fried in butter or broiled whole over the camp-fire.

But Chiquitito was not to be offered up as a sacrifice to any hungry stomach. Instead, he was allowed to wax fat and lazy with the crumbs which fell from his master's table, and when the army moved into the captured city of Santiago, the happy chicken was carried in state by a friendly orderly.

His new owner was attached to the general's staff, and when they moved into the government palace thither with the staff went his favored chickenship.

It was quite evident palaces had not been much in Chiquitito's line, but he soon fell into the exalted ways of his new station, and acted quite to the manor born.

When the American general and his staff were dining the chicken flew to the great man's shoulder and perched there with easy familiarity. Then, as his fancy moved him, he hopped from shoulder to shoulder of the junior officers, clinging to their epaulets, and pecking daintily at a morsel of cake or fruit held up by his obedient servant.

At night Chiquitito roosted in the chandelier of the great state chamber, and doubtless strange dreams harassed his chicken brain. If he could have spoken in our language he might have given us a good story of a Spanish vision or two which glided across the polished floor of the governor's apartment.

Somewhere in that deserted palace was found a gilded parrot's-cage, and forthwith it became the home of Chiquitito.

A few days before they took their departure from Santiago, the general and his aide were startled by a most extraordinary demonstration from their pet fowl.

" What's the matter with the creature? " laughed the general.

"I think high life must have turned his head," answered the puzzled officer.

"Chiquitito, Chiquitito!" cried a voice outside; and there, smiling more broadly than ever, was Jose, whose approach, unheard by the Americans, had been the cause of the joyous antics in the cage.

Quick as a flash, the officer held out the chicken through the open window.

"No, no," laughed the little boy; "bueno, bueno!" And, kissing his hand to his now important chick, he scudded off down the street; and that was indeed the last they saw of the little refugee.

His chickenship will live in peace and dignity on Governor's Island, a prize bird in many senses; and though he knows "mucho" about affairs in Santiago, he hasn't learned the English language, and couldn't if he would, tell his American friends long stories about those dreary days with Jose before the Americanos came to the sunny isle of Cuba.

Taming A Bear Cub

How an Alaska Indian Girl Accomplished a Feat Which Her Elders Wouldn't Undertake.

Stella Walthall Belcher

Youth's Companion. Reprinted in the
Montecello Express, Montecello, Iowa, May 31, 1900.

On the return trip of the steamer Pomona from the Alaska gold fields a brief stop was made at Juneau, where a polar bear cub was presented to the captain of the ship. He at once named it after the village whence it had come and chained it on the after deck for the amusement of the passengers.

Every one took great interest in the roly-poly stranger, as sundry scratched hands and legs soon bore testimony; but Juneau refused to be cultivated by the human family. She was a vicious little savage, snarling and snapping at every offer of peace and good will, until finally the passengers were glad to give her a wide berth.

We had a bright little Indian girl on board, however, who persisted in thrusting her friendship on Juneau. Her guardians, the missionaries, were prepared to see the cub give her a bad scratch, but it was soon evident that she was quite equal to caring for herself.

Each evening little Olga saved her dessert of fruit and cake, and fed it to the cub. Although Juneau ate the peace offering greedily, she still threatened her admirer with her claws. But Olga had a plan.

One day she cut an apple into tiny bits, and deliberately seated herself on the deck within the circle allowed to the cub. The very presumption of the act caused Miss Bruin to stand and stare while

Olga took the bits of apple and dropped them in a line, starting as near the cub as she could reach, and leading to her feet. Then she continued the apple line to her knee, and spreading out her skirt, dotted it here and there with the pieces. Several good-sized slices were saved for her arms and shoulder, and last, to top off, she placed the core on top of her head.

All this was done slowly and deliberately, and when it was finished Olga sat as still as a statue. Blinking and sniffing, the wily Juneau stole softly toward the apple line. The apple was juicy, and the bear put aside all fear and malice, and nibbled contentedly up to the two blunt little feet which were set up so sturdily before her. There the cub paused to study the silent figure, but finding that it did not move or offer to be friendly, she continued her feast.

Slowly and carefully she searched over the dress, not missing a morsel, and finally sniffed at the little girl's shoulder. Stepping gingerly into the soft lap, Juneau rose on her hind feet, rested her forepaws on Olga's chest, and hastily gulped down the remaining bits of apple until none was left but the tempting core on the child's head.

Then the bear, clinging with her sharp claws to the cloth jacket, climbed upon Olga's shoulder, clasped her round the neck for a balance, and nibbled the core.

I wondered if any of the grown-up white people on that ship could have sat so still. Our little passenger's courage never failed her. There was not the quiver of an eyelash to show that she was alive, and the wary cub, with a grunt of satisfaction, went back to her box to sleep. Not until then did the child move from her cramped position. Jumping up, she ran away full of glee to tell her friends.

Next day there was a large audience which stood at a respectful distance to watch the novel performance. The experiment of the day before was repeated with even greater success, for Juneau ended it that time by cuddling down in the soft, warm lap and going to sleep.

Of course these two little natives of Alaska became great friends, and when we docked at San Francisco the captain unchained the pretty cub, and put her into the arms of the only person who had had wit enough to tame her.

A NATIVE OF ALASKA.

God's Way

A Red Man's Solution of a Problem of Civilization

Stella Walthall Belcher

Collier's Magazine, April 13, 1907

Flat on the hard-packed threshold of her smokehouse sits Bridle-mouth Ann. Like the earth of her doorway she is sun-dried. The skin of her face has the juiceless crinkled appearance of grayish brown crape, but under the thin glazed surface of two deep scars, that run bridle-like from the corners of her mouth to the shadows of her ears, is a purplish hue of blood, the only life-color left in a creature who is ashen and age-shriveled.

On the right of Bridle-mouth Ann crouches a lean, stiff-haired, tawny dog of wolfish head, whose ears prick and droop, and whose nostrils quiver with each passing tale in the hot north wind. About the woman and her dog lies an aura of hopelessness. It strikes the mind as forcibly as the desolation of her home salutes the eye. Tomorrow, and the next day, and the next is the same to her. Those whom she loved have passed on. She sits and looks and looks across the clay-colored river, but what she sees exists within.

It was not always so. Once she was a handsome, laughter-loving, young squaw. The strong, sun-browned men in uniforms called her "Merry" Ann. That was before they took their guns and horses across the mountains to stay, and when the place we call "campus" was still "parade."

They will tell you at Captain John's Rancheria that they remember the day when the bridle was put in Ann's mouth by Sochtish, oldest chief of the Hupas. Between the time when Ann

131

was "Merry" and the day when she was made "Bridle-mouth" runs the story.

Ann's smoke-house, as now, was one of a dozen squat hovels that clustered on the bleached shoulder of a bluff across the river from the post. There the filarial grew fine and soft like fur, and ran in flattened, shimmering waves before each breath of the hills. An arrow's flight from the smoke-house on the highest point of the bluff, where rocks outnumbered grass-blades, sprawled Captain John's sweat-house, an excrescence of rough-hewn timber and river-polished stones.

In the season when daylight hours were long and cloudless, and brilliant blue lizards flashed in and out among the hot stones, Jimmy, Ann's youngest son, made the little rock-bound terrace of the sweat-house his dream place. Thither his mother always followed him, seeking to make his thoughts her thoughts. He was unlike her sons George and Thomas, who attended school across the Oregon line, and her heart was troubled for fear Injun devil tormented the body of her littlest boy.

"Does mother's heart dream sweet dreams?" she asked him for the hundredth time—yea, the ten hundredth. The boy crept close this day and rested his head against her low-hanging breast. His eyes reached across the clay-colored river to the Digger pines that wigwagged in the hot north wind.

"I dream that I have the sweetness of honey in my heart, and I hear words that have never been spoken in the smoke-house, and I have the smell of wild honeysuckle in my nostrils."

"Haät-now, haät-now," crooned Ann, swaying gently back and forth as if to lull her anxious thoughts, "tell me more of thy dreams."

"I would not be like my brothers. They are dirty and lazy," he murmured. "It will be pleasant when I am old enough to lie all night in the sweat-house and rise in the gray light and run to the river and swim till I am clean, like the white of thine eye, oh, mother. Then I shall have a sound in my ears like the wind blowing against a long horse-hair and I shall feel that I am strong inside."

The warm glow of fancy gave his eyes a tender, mysterious light that troubled Merry Ann's heart.

"Ah, sweet hope of my life," she whispered, "thou dreamiest strange dreams and thou hast strange desires. Thou shalt not go to school like thy brothers. The school men would sap thy strength as the north wind saps the milk of the young wheat. Thou shalt not go. I have said."

Contented with her promise, the boy' head became heavy on his mother's breast. She looked into his face and saw that he slept. Very gently she laid him down and, returning to the smoke-house, took a basket of acorn meal on her back and went down to the river bank below the bluff to leach it in the sand.

The stillness of old age was over the Rancheria. The able-bodied women were at their teaching, and the bucks watched the nets on the fish dam a half-hour's walk up the river. In this treeless abode nothing moved but the furry grass and the garments of the dead that swung silently from the frames over the graves.

Into this still place came a white man, driving across the bluff and leaving a double track of broken stalks through the crisp grass. He stopped near the smoke-house and stood up in his buggy to look for dogs that bite before they bark. From his elevated place the man saw the sleeping lad. He fastened the lines behind the whip, sprang out, and walked briskly to the sweat-house.

The boy did not wake till he felt a strong arm holding him. Then something inside rose like a great wind that blew him hither and thither, a creature of nails, teeth, and kicking legs. But the strong man climbed into the buggy with his prize and drove away. While he forded the river and drove up the road to the whitewashed fence on the other side he held the boy between his knees as in a vise. At the platform stile the man took the fighting, struggling creature in his arms, face down, and crossed the campus to a long low white building used as a dormitory.

At the sound of the quick footstep on the gravel a woman, who had been reading on the veranda, started up from her chair.

"I've brought Merry Ann's boy alive," announced the man, letting Jimmy slip to the ground and pinning him there by the shoulders. "Subdue him if you can before his mother comes."

The woman went down the steps and reached forth to take the boy by the arm. She gave a cry of pain. Her fingers were caught. Two rows of glistening teeth were clenched upon her anemic flesh.

"You little savage!" ejaculated the man, and shook the boy off as he would a dog.

But the woman's hands had turned to claws and she whisked the boy up the steps and through the door before he could plan another attack. Inside the house a baptism of soap and water was administered to Jimmy. From an eruptive youngster of dangerous activity he was transformed into a smoldering volcano of outraged pride. He permitted himself to be clothed in garments several sizes too large for him and to be led out on the veranda. With one little hot restless hand imprisoned in the woman's he stood at her side and looked down at his mother and his grandfather, Captain John, who had come while he was undergoing transformation, and were standing patiently at the foot of the steps.

Merry Ann wore her red and white calico dress of state. Her hat was a cast-off thing of rusty brown straw and faded red ribbon, and bore two faded feathers. The sight of this hat inspired Jimmy with more respect than all the school man's arts.

Apart from Ann stood Captain John, his shrunken overalls and bare feet presenting an irreverent contrast to his patriarchal white hair; and leaning against the frame of a nearby swing was the school superintendent.

"Well, what does Merry Ann think about it?" asked the latter.

"Yo know Merry Ann she no lik huh boy come to school," exclaimed Captain John. "Maybeso he larn damnbad nonsense. Yes, sir-mam, she tink he git it saick. She tink maybeso Jimmy have Injun devil in he belly. What yo say?"

The man muttered something intended for the ears of the woman on the veranda about Jimmy having more than one devil—one for each leg and arm—but Captain John was not skilled beyond a few sentences in the white man's language, and stopped to ponder.

"Go on, go on," commanded the superintendent impatiently. "Tell Merry Ann that the government requires her to send her boy to school. It's nothing to me. I have to do what the Government tells me to do. Tell her she'll have to submit—give in—be good Injun."

With his back toward the woman Captain John talked into space in front of him. He said a few words and waited. Then he said a few more words very cautiously, as if speech were a fragile thing not to be used carelessly. The silences were weighty. It took an hour, but, at last, sounds clicked in Merry Ann's glottis and rolled from under her tongue like thick oil. She had signified consent.

Without looking up or appearing to notice the child on the veranda or the school man, she crossed the campus and passed out of sight, always moving with a teetering trot as if she carried a heavy forward burden that made her little feet hurry to preserve her balance.

Jimmy slept in the woods that night and for three nights thereafter, because the windows of the dormitory had not been strong or high enough. The two lazy policemen found him in the burnt-out hollow of a stump, half-starved, but fierce as a young bobcat. They dragged him back to be rebaptized in soap and water. In the next five years Jimmy was a terror to his kind as well as to the school men. It was a rare occurrence to have a full roll-call. Some boy was generally missing: in the infirmary, it was said, with a broken arm or a bruised shin or a black eye—because of Injun Jim. Living in the Hupa Reservation, outside the little circle of well-intentioned men and women, cogs and wheels to the machinery of a Government school, was one man who had a kinship with all wild and untamed creatures. Outwardly he was the apotheosis of tameness—small, bent-shouldered, thin-whiskered, bespectacled, slow of speech, and yet the other nature of him, which he had grilled into outward subjection, was akin to Injun Jim's. In the man of God was also to be found a man of earth.

It was the missionary's habit to sit unobserved near an open window that commanded the school-yard. He discovered very soon that Injun Jim was always an observer and never a participant in the games. The boy gazed at his fellows with a from-under stare that was somber and mysterious. It was evident to the watcher at the window that Jimmy only broke away from his reserve when he was impelled by a positive motive. His particular animus was oftenest aroused by some big hulking bully, who crossed the campus only to leave behind him a wake of blubbering, whimpering boys. This sight invariably brought Jimmy to his feet. With stiff hanging arms and clenched fists he had a brief struggle between his desire for justice and his Indian reserve; that over, he threw out his arms and plunged into the bully.

Five times the trees flowered and fruited, and the nuts ripened in the woods while the missionary wrestled with his God for some sign of redemption in the boy. He of all the people in the reservation saw the inner struggle between right and wrong that was forever going on. He was the only one who knew that, as often as Jimmy was torn to mend his ways, he slipped off the campus to be gone for hours, sometimes for days. None but the man of God knew where he went. He had followed Jimmy to his secret nook in the woods and discovered that the boy played a fiddle acquired by some means known to the devil that was said to possess him. His music he created as he played. It came from the fullness of his desires, a weird string of sounds without melody or rhythm.

One day this wild somber boy, now little less than a man, sat in his nook fiddling softy with no thought of the instrument in hand, but letting his soul run free with the sounds. Without warning a creature, clad in white from her little shoes to her flapping hat, stepped into this sacred nook. Out of bright china-blue eyes she looked into the somber eyes of the boy. Neither moved till the bow slipped out of Jimmy's loosened fingers and rattled to the ground. He was unconscious of self, of everything, only that he saw something in those china-blue eyes that made something in his breast leap like a living creature.

A sweet smile dimpled the young girl's face. "I am the superintendent's daughter," she said naively, as if that fact would warrant her intrusion. Sitting down on the moss-covered log, she spread out her skirts daintily. "I came to Hupa only yesterday. When I heard you playing I thought I would like to know who it was. I am fond of music. Won't you play again, please?"

He was looking into her eyes wistfully, but at her request took his bow and began a wild throbbing chain of sounds that was like a voice speaking. Tears came into the blue eyes. Jimmy stopped with a twanging discord.

"It makes my heart ache," she sighed. "What is the name of this strange music?"

"I don't know," he answered. "It is what I feel."

"Where did you get the fiddle?" she asked.

"I stole it," he replied, just above a whisper. "Down there they call me Injun Jim. I steal, I lie, I do what I please."

A cloud drifted across the girl's eyes, and she looked away with a little shiver.

"Oh, how wicked!" she breathed.

"The fiddle belonged to a man who didn't have sense enough to play it," he began to explain.

"But that is all very wrong," she reproved gently. "You won't do it any more, will you? Please, promise me."

"No," he whispered after a long silence, "not any more."

It was twilight when Jimmy and the young girl went down to the campus. They parted at the stile. He continued to the river, crossed it in a canoe, thence up the bluff to the sweat-house. Throwing himself down on the terrace, he lay with his face upturned to the darkening sky and waited. In six years he had not returned to the Rancheria, though it was within an hour's walk of the campus, and no thought of home had taken him across the river that night.

It was quite dark when Jimmy heard the soft pad-pad of bare feet, and as Captain John, stripped for the night, stopped above him, he sat up and addressed him in the language of the smoke-house.

"I have come to ask why I am called James Stuart, and my fat brother, who lives at Klamath, George Matilton, and the one who is a packer, Thomas Campbell? Why do we three have different names?"

The old indian spoke with many pauses. A few words, then a long-drawn breath, and a long wait.

"Thomas is the son of Campbell, he that was of the full blood. He was thy mother's man. Campbell was a great hunter in the days when the blood runs hot and fast. Thy mother was lonely when he was away.... So thy brother George is the son of Matilton, the gold digger.... But thou art James Stuart, because thy father was Lieutenant James Stuart, who went away with the soldiers. It is the custom of my people to name the child after the father."

The old man stooped to the small polished entrance, and his shriveled old body shot down into the blackness and heat of the sweat-house like a huge amphibian diving into the water.

The morning light was over the valley when Jimmy crossed the campus to the dormitory. As the boys came out he joined the line at the end. No comment was made on his absence. It would be reported as usual, but demerits did not count against a boy who had never received a merit. That evening after the day's work was over the teachers met on the campus. They talked of one subject. "Injun Jim was perfect in all his lessons to-day." "Injun Jim received full credits for good behavior to-day." "Injun Jim stood at the head for cleanliness to-day."

Day after day the boy, who was more and more like a man, went to the nook with his fiddle under his arm and played. One day he heard steps on the leaf carpet that were heavier and yet softer than those of his little wild friends. He clutched his fiddle to his breast and watched the parting bushes with glad shining eyes. When Flora was seated at his side he laid his slim brown hand alongside hers on the log.

"I am a half-breed," he said. "I wonder which is stronger in me, the Indian or the white man?"

"The white man in you is strongest," she answered positively.

"How do you know?" he queried.

"I read it in your speech and your quickness to understand. Last night I heard them say down at my father's house that you stood first in all your classes. If you continue they will send you to Carlisle at the end of the year."

He gave her a flash of grateful eyes.

"When I was a child I dreamed things that never happened in the smoke-house," he said thoughtfully. "And now I would often obey the teachers for the soft feeling in my heart, but something calls me away to be in the sun all day and do nothing but eat and sleep. But there is another part of me, which will not let me rest, and drives me back to the school whether I will it or not. This part of me would know all that is to be found in books. When I run away I say I don't care, but I do. I come back. And now every day I ask myself many times which is stronger in me, the idle ungrateful part, or that which would do the will of the school men?"

"I wish I could tell you," murmured Flora. "I know that you are different. I feel it when you play your fiddle."

In the course of the next week Jimmy discovered a power within himself that made his heart swell with joy. The meetings between Flora and himself were no longer subject to chance. When he bade her come by means of his fiddle straightway she came. They talked of themselves at these meetings, but there came a day when he only played to her. The music told his story better than words. He played to her till her china-blue eyes were soft like flowers, and her head drooped and rested on his shoulder.

At her touch Jimmy started up shaken as with a chill. That part of him which defied the school men had bidden the girl to his arms, but at her touch the other nature, which stood for justice, came on like water rising in a well and could not be stopped. The struggle was brief. A moment later he was flying down the hill alone.

He did not call Flora again while he was able to reason, but one day he forgot and let the strings speak for him. She came smiling at him across the parted bushes. All athirst for her he dropped his fiddle and called her to his arms.

On this day the missionary was following his bent of walking through the woods, and, of a sudden, stepped into the little nook. The sight that met his gaze struck him as a blow. Standing in the open space were Jimmy and Flora, the dark hair of the boy mingled with the blond hair of the girl, the dark cheek pressed against the fair cheek, and two strong arms like bars across the slim young back. The boy raised his head at the movement in the brush, and the man met the challenge of his eyes.

That night from his window the missionary beckoned Jimmy to his room.

"My boy," he began as he polished his spectacles painstakingly, "I would like you to explain the meaning of what I saw to-day."

Jimmy's head tilted back, and his eyes expanded and took in light, but still he was silent.

"Let me answer for you, my boy," the man went on. "You and Flora have gotten to love one another, and you were telling her. Am I right?"

The sight of the boy's tightly closed lips was vexing.

"He's all Indian," the man told himself regretfully. "I'm afraid I'll never reach him."

"If this friendship continues it must end in marriage," he went on aloud. "Marriage is right in God's sight when two people are rightly mated, but in this case it would be a great wrong. Flora's father expects her to return to her people in the East. She belongs there. She has no place in this rough, primitive life. But she loves you as many a girl has loved a boy before. She finds you different from all the others. You have a heritage that makes you so. Your father, James Stuart, is a colonel in the army. His mother, your grandmother, was a saint. Jimmy because of the good white blood in your veins you should be manly and generous. You should protect the weak and not take advantage. You should love fair play."

The boy's eyes were pinched together with a look of pain, and on either side near the temples was a spot of reflected light that gave his forehead a luminous quality almost unearthly. As he had listened a look of anguish had come into his eyes. The missionary's heart throbbed in sympathy.

"It will be best for her to break away," said the boy.

"I doubt if she can do that," interposed the other. "She would go to the end of the earth with you now. You must be the one to break away."

"I will never do it," cried Jimmy, starting up.

"Then her father will have to know," said the old man.

"It might make trouble for her," Jimmy put in hastily. "Maybe in a little while she will give me up." His hand was on the doorknob.

"Stay, let us talk it over, my boy," pleaded the man.

But Jimmy went out into the twilight.

The bell had called the older pupils to study hour and the campus was still and deserted. Jimmy should have been bending over his books, but he turned away from the school building and followed an irrigating ditch up into the woods to where it leaped a full-grown stream from the flume.

"Jimmy," called a voice from below. "Jimmy, are you up there?"

He scrambled down the steep bank, the dead madroño leaves rattling about him like rain.

With a little startled cry Flora reached out her arms, but Jimmy caught them, and held her firmly away. For a minute he tried to master his voice, and then – "Would you marry a half-breed and give up going back to your home?" he whispered.

"I would give up everything for you," she answered, her head drooping against his arm.

"What if I should steal again, Flora? The Indian flesh is weak. What if I should be dirty like old Mike? What if I should get drunk like Sochtish?"

"Why do you vex me with these questions?" she fretted. "It isn't right. You couldn't be like Mike or Sochtish." Her voice broke in a sob.

Jimmy allowed her to take his hand and half pull him down the hill. At first she coaxed him on, but finding that he hung back, she became petulant.

"Oh, I don't understand you. For some reason you are different to-day. Please, tell me what is the matter." She put up her hand impulsively and drew his face down close to hers to see if he were in earnest. His troubled gaze met hers.

"Kiss me, Jimmy," she pleaded. "You have never kissed me."

The blood sprang to the boy's face and the warmth of it entered his eyes. They expanded and shone on her like twin stars. With swift outstretched arms he gathered her to his breast and kissed her on the mouth with a long stifling pressure.

"Jimmy—Jimmy—don't—" He cut off her words. Another long clinging kiss and another and another fell full on her lips. Panting and frightened at his vehemence, she sank limply in his arms. He let her go as suddenly as he had taken her. She staggered back into a chaparral bush, clutching at the thorny branches for support and sobbing out her futile protest: "Don't—don't—"

He had disappeared in the woods before she realized that she was alone.

"Jimmy," she called, "Jimmy, I don't care—I'm not angry."

But no answer came, and, clasping her hot cheeks with both hands, she ran down to the kitchen door of her father's house and through the deserted rooms to her own little chamber. There she fell on her knees by the bed, her maiden soul stirred to its depths by the joy and fear of those burning kisses.

Through the underbrush the boy took his course straight to the nook above. His hands were clenched at his side. His feet sprang from the ground like winged creatures. His heart was pounding in his breast, in his ears, in his throat. Frenzied with the call of his heart, he threw himself full-length on the cool, moss-grown log. His energy was spent in an ecstasy of grief. He lay for hours like one who has crawled out of a terrible, menacing danger more dead than alive. In the hour of mountain dawn the other nature awoke and reasoned with him.

Before the week was over the teachers told each other that Jimmy had lost his chance for Carlisle. Offenses were not stated. There were sins of omission and commission, most of them unpardonable. Flora heard these rumors from different sources and sought Jimmy in the woods and on the campus, but he slipped away from her only passing near enough once or twice to let her see that his clothes were untidy and his hands and face dirty and grimy. These signs of backsliding sent a foreboding fear to pluck at her heart along with sorrow and wounded pride. Her belief in Jimmy was shaken. Could she have seen his eyes, his eyes that followed her like a famished dog—but he always looked the other way when she could have seen. Once he let her meet him under the trees. She did not try to control the tears that flushed her eyes.

"They—they say you've lost your chance for Carlisle," she quavered, with trembling underlip.

"What's the use?" he mumbled, his hungry eyes averted from her piteously crumpled face. "I don't want any half-white education. Give me all Indian. We're bound to come back sooner or later."

After that as often as Jimmy saw Flora on the campus he took that opportunity to waylay some smaller boy and badger him into a state of whimpering anger. And that was not all. He was dirty. He was quarrelsome. He was the constant source of disturbance in the chapel and the schoolroom.

The missionary found it hard to get close to him, but one day, making a point of it, he met Jimmy at the dining-room door.

"I'm bitterly disappointed in you, my boy," he began. "Has all my teaching been in vain? Why don't you keep your promise with me about Flora?"

"It takes longer than I thought," muttered Jimmy. "Give me another day. Then she'll be glad to see the last of me."

On the morrow, which was the Sabbath, Jimmy was seen to ride out of the reservation. He had no permission, but he was a law unto himself. At eleven the children and older pupils assembled in the chapel across the road to listen to the missionary's service. Flora was of the number that came to worship, but her restless eyes persistently sought the place where Jimmy was supposed to sit. After the service she stood near the outside steps with her father, watching the children march to the campus.

The road was spanned with a double line of boys and girls, keeping time to the jangling beat of a triangle. All at once some one shouted a warning. A man on horseback was bearing down on the children from the main road. Just in front of the chapel where Flora and her father stood the animal was brought to a halt.

A hundred pairs of upturned eyes were on the rider. The slouching figure lurched from side to side, but the legs, bending back at the knees and clinging to the horse's lathered sides, preserved his balance.

It was Injun Jim, hatless, coatless, dirty; veins of sweat starting from under his matted hair and draining across his cheeks into the grime of his neck. It was Jimmy, stripped of the glamour of good looks and decency.

The boy broke into a loud, hoarse guffaw. He mixed the tongue of the smoke-house and the school man. As the superintendent started forward with an angry exclamation to put an end to the disgraceful scene, Jimmy pulled a protruding bottle from his pocket and twirled it overhead threateningly. Straight against the chapel wall he hurled it. With the crash of glass and the rattle of boards a great ragged patch of moisture appeared on the thirsty wall, and the pungent smell of cheap whisky filled the air. A look of aversion and disgust was on the faces of the teachers, but Jimmy's hungry eyes were only for Flora.

Late that evening when the campus was deserted, and the irrigating ditches ran with quicksilver of the moon's making, Flora slipped out of her father's house and sought the missionary.

"I want to tell somebody, and I dare not tell father, he is so angry with Jimmy," she sobbed. "I don't understand how it happened, but Jimmy drew my heart away from me, and I knew that it belonged to him. He seemed so good and strong, but he wasn't—he wasn't. I never want to see him again. I'm going away tomorrow morning with father. I'll never come back."

"It is better so, my child," said the man.

A week later the missionary went to see Jimmy in the rancheria across the river. He found him lying on the terrace of the sweathouse that had been Captain John's before he went to his long home inside the little picket fence. The old man studied the boy a long time in silence. Why should a drunken boy have sober, hungry-looking eyes? But standing there before Jimmy, a great light came to him. He was answered.

When he had gone slowly across the bluff, Ann came with her teetering trot down to the terrace and tried again to make her boy's thoughts her thoughts.

"I wore the wild honeysuckle on my heart," he told her, "and it made me glad and strong. But the north wind blew it away. Now that I have conquered that other part of me I am heavy-hearted, oh, mother...I wonder if the place where Captain John has gone—"

"Hush—hush—" whispered Ann, stricken with fear. "Thou shalt not take the name of the dead in vain."

The habit of the sweat-house, that had prolonged the life of Captain John beyond his fellows, found a weak spot in the constitution of the half-breed boy. The sweating at night took his strength, and the plunge in the clay-colored river chilled him. All day long he lay on the terrace like a wilted cornstalk.

The morning came when he did not return from his dip in the river. Hours later two men from another rancheria came across the furry grass carrying between them the slender naked body of a youth. They laid it on the terrace of the sweat-house. They said they had found it on the river bank, caught in a net of willow roots. And Ann came with the skulking stiff-haired dog at her side and looked. Then tearing her long black hair out of its braids she called down curses on the school men, and on the school that had sapped the strength of her boy; she called down curses on the river and the sweat-house; she threw her heavy body against the picket fence that enclosed her father's grave and cursed the sacred dead. Because of him the school men had had their way with her boy. In that black hour, when all her friends stood away from her appalled, came Sochtish, oldest chief of the Hupas. He dragged Ann to the fence and pressed her head back against the pickets and held her there as in a vise. With his long, sharp knife he made a backward slash that slit her mouth from ear to ear. She dropped away from his hand like a sack of meal. Very carefully he wiped and resheathed his knife.

"That is the way the tribe punishes the Indian that breaks the law and takes the name of the dead in vain!" he proclaimed.

That was twenty years ago. Ann still wears her bridle and waits; the dog crouches beside her with his sphinx-like head and sniffs the tales in the hot north wind.

NOTE: According to an article in the Arcata Union on April 30, 1907:

The story was submitted to Colliers in the prize story contest held some months ago, and while not a prize winner, the production was accepted and the talented writer received $450 for it....From a literary standpoint the story is well told, the descriptions showing that the writer was familiar with her locations and characters. The only incident in the story that is founded on facts is the story of Bridle Mouth Anne. The mutilation of the squaw actually took place, but was done when she was about 12 years of age, and an Indian named Senichson, who was known as a bad Indian committed the deed. According to Indian custom, a fire is kept burning on the grave of the dead for a stated number of days after death, which is a period of mourning, during which time the relatives may be consoled. After the fire has been allowed to go out, it is a mortal insult to even speak of the name of the dead, and for this breech of the tribal laws, the Indian child was frightfully mutilated.

Captain John's sweat house   Lismer Family

Madam

Stella Walthall

The California and Overland Monthly, v.67, May, 1916, p. 401.

It is a matter of tradition in Trinity County, that wild, picturesque, almost roadless country in the North, that Madam was
handsome and gay, and a good comrade. That she was given
to garishness in dress and had a loud, hearty voice that would
have been unseemly in polished society was of no importance in
the early fifties, when Madam was having "her day." What was
more to the point with the miners was her unfailing generosity
and kindness. Men speak of her even to this day with an accent
of respect.

Madam certainly understood men and fairly earned her popu-
larity. She made pies for them when they were homesick; nursed
them when they were bruised and broken, and helped make their
coffins when that was all they needed. And being young and gay,
and unfettered by conventions, she shared in their drunken revels.
That was when the Bar was a bustling mining community and
hundreds of pioneers washed and rocked for gold. Being a lone
woman among many men she was weaker and stronger than
other women of her class, and in proportion paid penalty for her
shortcomings like a man, and took her praise and adulation like
a very feminine woman.

There are some facts in this story, if we are to believe the
testimony of the oldest inhabitant. And some fiction. I, also,
refer you to the oldest inhabitant. When Scotty of Hoopa gravely
assures me that he helped bury "tha puir woman and her saix
children side by side with her puir dead husband," and on the
other hand "Chicken Masten" asserts with heat that "the Madam

never had chick nor child never had a husband only a dawg" I am constrained to admit that history of the early fifties in Trinity County is a composite.

It is not necessary to dip into Madam's story prior to her advent on the Trinity. Her past as it was told to me may be pure fiction. Facts begin to illuminate the trail when Juan 'Zapisto bore down on the community with his burro and his Mexican hairless dog.

Madam had just stepped out of the house to gather the late Castillian roses that she had coaxed through a hot summer when Juan and his dog came round the corner. Chihuahua flew at the woman's skirts, capering like a mad thing. Instantly she swung him up in her arms, taking the frantic kisses as a matter of course.

"Where did you get him? Such a darling! See how he loves me already the poor, shivery, little beast!"

Don Juan (the miners had promptly tacked on the title) made her a grave, respectful salutation with his big sombrero. His well bred air distinguished him as a gentleman, a romantic, ne'er-do-well sort of gentleman who would not be overfond of work, but would glory in an adventure that would wear him to the bone.

Madam instinctively paid tribute. She smoothed some stray locks that hung around her ears, and under cover of the little dog, pulled the neck of her waist together. "I am pleased that you like my little dog," said Zapisto. "I brought him all the way from San Diego with me. He is a devoted little creature."

"That is often the way," sighed Madam. "These little dogs will do so much for us, and I'll venture that the miners give him many a sly kick just because he is so little and helpless. Come into the house, won't you," she added. "I want to give him a bit of venison."

Anything small and helpless appealed to Madam's maternal instinct, and it amused the men to see her motherly solicitude while the little dog ate. Don Juan stood near, politely smiling and listening with evident pleasure to the feminine chatter. A few hours later he strolled away with some provisions under his arm.

Madam followed him to the door. She was subdued in manner to suit the manner of the man. Trust Madam for that. After he was gone, she stood there a long time, but her eyes followed him until he disappeared in the dense woods beyond the clearing.

She was observed, of course. A dozen men were lounging inside the big room, which was saloon, living-room, store and post office. Above was an attic where the men slept, and at one side was a lean-to kitchen with a curtained-off recess for Madam. She must have endured many hardships in that kitchen and seen some sights that would have frozen the blood of a less virile woman, but, history mellowed by age, kindly softens these facts in Madam's life.

After a few weeks Don Juan was coming daily to the log house, ostensibly to get provisions, and Madam no longer was careless about her dress. She spent hours in patching her worn clothing, and in arranging her hair in a fashionable waterfall. Their friendship ripened like the late peaches all in a day, and its possibilities was the principal theme of conversation in the camp.

Late in the summer, however, more serious business was afoot than watching a rival. The long-suffering Indians had risen against the whites. Far-seeing men had expected this reckoning day. And it came as they prophesied, with burning and killing. The word of it traveled hot-footed down the trail.

Before the whites had time to see their danger they were cut off from the coast. Fort Humboldt was garrisoned with soldiers, but between the bar on the Trinity and the fort spread a chain of high mountains which made an effectual barrier against a rapid retreat. The trail to the southeast was alive with hostile Indians, and the only other outlet was by the way of New River. Some of the miners had already started in that direction. Most of the men as they passed the log house stopped and tried to persuade Madam to go with them. They had a genuine friendship for this comrade, and wanted to help her, but Madam lingered. She pretended not to believe the reports.

One morning during the excitement Don Juan came to the house with his little dog.

"I want to leave Chihuahua here with you," he said. "Some of us are going across the Trinity on a scouting trip. It's a great chance to see what is going on over there. I'll be back tonight for Chihuahua. Adios, amiga mia."

Madam followed him outside the house.

"Juan," she whispered, "don't go for my sake, don't go. Come with me by the way of New River. The Indians are friendly that way. I am afraid something will happen to you over there."

"There is no danger. Nothing could happen to me," protested Juan. "Keep out of danger yourself, querida amiga mia."

Suddenly Madam stretched out her arms to the man. Her coarse, handsome face was convulsed and white.

"But Juan," she pleaded, "I can't let you go. I love you better than my life. I want you to come with me and have a respectable home somewhere. I am dead tired of this."

The Spaniard took her trembling hands and pressed them to his heart.

"Madam, you do me great honor." He addressed her with all the respect that he would have used to a queen. "To be loved by you is supreme happiness. I love you, querida. You are the flower of my heart. But" he drew himself up proudly, "ten years ago I was married to the Señorita Carmen Vallejo of San Francisco."

For an unforgettable moment they gazed in one another's eyes. Juan made a movement as if to take her in his arms, but Madam covered her face with her hands, and half blindly made her way into the lean-to.

Later in the day some men rushed in with the news that the Indians had burned the ranch a few miles up the river, and had made threats to burn the house at the Bar and murder every white man in the community.

It was strange to see the matter of fact way in which Madam received the news. She stood calmly by while the men got together the packs which they intended to carry on their backs.

They one and all took it for granted that she would go with them. But when they were ready to leave she insisted that there was no danger, and that she would wait until evening.

The men were exasperated at what they called "damned contrariness." Two of them half-dragged her out of the house and tried to force her up the trail. She was struggling furiously to get away when a man came running after them.

"Zapisto was killed just now across the river," he panted. "The devils will catch us if we don't hurry. For God's sake, woman, come along! Don't hold us back!"

Madam's taut muscles suddenly relaxed. For a moment they thought she would faint, but it was only a passing weakness. She pulled herself together, and meekly fell into the step of the man who clutched her arm. Her bent shoulders and drooping head conveyed a poignant sense of woe to the soft-hearted miners. When her feet now and then slipped on the sharp rocks in the trail they reached involuntary aid, and talked of her in hushed whispers among themselves.

As evening came on they made camp in a deserted shack. The owner was ahead on the trail. Madam refused to eat the food they offered her, and sat apart, white and silent, while the men made their plans for the night. One of them tossed her a blanket and went to bed in the corner with his arms for a pillow. A night guard was dispensed with, and most of the men made their beds on the ground outside the shack.

Madam crept under the blanket and made a feint of sleeping. After a while, convinced that none of the men were awake, she stole out of the cabin and ran down the trail that led to the Bar. She never looked back to see if she were followed. Her knowledge of men was sure. She reasoned that when they found that she had really slipped away that they would curse a little and give it up as a thankless job.

The bar was ten miles away. It was too dark to see the trail, but the going was easily down hill, and Madam swung along at a running gait. At a little past midnight she came to the foot of the trail. The log house was dark, and apparently deserted, but a small piercing sound answered her straining ears. Madam fully realized her danger as she paused for a moment at the edge of the clearing to satisfy herself that no other sounds were coming from the house. She knew it was possible that some of the Indians had broken into the big room and gotten the liquors under the saloon bar, but in that event they would be on the floor in a drunken stupor. The greatest danger lurked in the shadow of the dense woods. There was no time to hesitate. Gathering up her full skirts. Madam ran swiftly to the kitchen door, and pushing it open noiselessly, caught the little hairless dog in her arms.

Several times on the trail she had spoken to the men about the dog. They had laughed at her in derision. The Indians would burn the house and the dog in it, they comforted her. The beast would never have a chance to starve to death. Madam was not an imaginative person, but the vision of Chihuahua gnawing out his vitals was unbearable.

Ominous sounds coming across the clearing roused Madam to immediate action. It was a case now of running for her life. Snatching a blanket from the bed, she wrapped the dog in it, and slipped out of the house and into the nearest brush thicket. For a moment she stood quivering with fear. She knew that the quick ear of the Indians would catch the smallest sound of snapping twigs, and that they would follow that sound with unerring instinct.

She began making her way through the brush, cautiously, with the idea of reaching the spring at the foot of the hill. When at last she felt the moist earth give under her feet, she dropped into the tangle of ferns and undergrowth and tore it away with her free hand till she touched water. Then, plunging her face into it again and again, something of its coolness entered her fevered blood.

She had not taken thought of food or drink since she had heard of Juan's death. The terrible void in her did not clamor for food or drink. Holding Chihuahua close she broke into dry, noiseless sobs. How near and sweet and brief happiness had been! Why should she fear death? Had she not reached the zenith of her life when she loved a man for himself?

But after all, self-preservation is an animal instinct, and though Madam reasoned, she did not reassure herself. The first yell of the Indians sent a thrill of sickening fear over her. Very soon flecks of blood red light came dancing into her retreat, and the sound of crackling flames made the dog squirm on her arm. She hushed him, and wrapped him closer in the blanket. His warm little body gave a sense of comfort to her quivering nerves. In the hours of waiting for the Indians to finish their work of revenge she fell into a stupor, which was broken by the crash of timber and shouts of drunken revelry.

Madam believed that they would soon leave the smouldering ruins and start in pursuit of the miners. It seemed to her wholly improbable that they would pass the spring, hidden as it was in the undergrowth, but she was also aware that Indians act on instincts peculiar to themselves. She did not comfort herself with any sense of false security. Her ears were strained for every tell tale sound, and when she heard voices coming in her direction she huddled closer to the ground in breathless fear. In those tense moments when the Indians were passing, the strong passion-scarred woman sounded the depths of her sordid life. Incidents that had long since passed out of memory, suddenly stood out before her. Two men that had fought bare-handed to their death for her, she had cared for neither of them, had cast off their memory as easily as a falling leaf. Now she shuddered, and long-delayed shame and regret welled up from the depths of her and made her rock to and fro in miserable penitence.

The guttural voices trailed into the distance, and melted into the roar of the river. The stillness was ominous, and Madam was painfully alert again. Half-formed questions raced through her mind. Why had the Indians come that way? What were they looking for? Where had they gone? Madam drew a painful breath and cautiously straightened out her cramped arms and legs. Every muscle ached. And little Chihuahua she had held him so close he must be half-smothered. She carefully unwrapped the blanket and let it fall away from him.

The little beast covered her hands with kisses as he struggled to get down. All at once he stiffened in her arms. Madam was looking into blackness, but she knew the dog had seen. With a startled gasp she dropped back on the ground. But Chihuahua knew his duty and broke into the sharp yap of his kind.

Instantly a huge body plunged into the thicket. With a guttural yell, the grapevines were torn apart and the dull light from the smouldering ruins fell on Madam and the barking dog.

* * * *

A few days later some miners who had come out of hiding found the bodies of Madam Weaver and the little dog at the spring. Madam's scalp was dangling at an Indian's belt.

* * * *

When you motor along the new Trinity highway this coming year or the next year, they will show you the spring where Madam gave up her life for the little dog, and will tell you, perhaps, that my story is mostly fiction. I am not so sure. As Don Juan would have said: Quien sabe. Sabe Dios.

Three Minutes with a Panther

Short Stories in, Adventurers All
February 25, 1933 Pp 141-142

Note: The stories submitted for this publication were supposed to be true stories, so this may be the true story of how Stella killed a panther. It does fit the information given to us by Edward C. Waterman.

A story of one thousand words doesn't leave any room for details or fine writing. One must stick to the unvarnished tale. This adventure took place in three minutes of actual time. It will take three minutes of your time to read it—if you read as you run.

It is not uncommon for women to kill panthers in Northern California where I live. Generally they have the use of a full-sized fire arm and a man to aid them on the side. In my case I had neither.

I had gone to our log cabin on Trinity Summit for a vacation and was accompanied by my small boy and his chum. Two pups, greatly beloved by my family, were to be our protection against imaginary dangers. Real danger was not to be considered. The pups slept out in the small enclosed yard, while the boys and I occupied bunks in the cabin. A long window close to my corner bunk looked out on the meadow without intervening fence. The one door opened onto the yard without benefit of doorstep.

We went to bed soon after dark but I was a long time getting to sleep. The pups kept rushing out on the meadow, barking timorously an then ki-yi-ing back to safety in the yard. Coyotes I thought to myself. Finally I dropped off.

I was startled out of my first deep sleep by a stampede of horses and mules. With bells clanking, animals snorting and squealing, the whole bunch galloped right up to the window, one mare in particular running her nose along the window pane. I jumped up screaming and frightened them away. They continued their mad rush out into the woods.

As I dropped down on my bed again I heard a low growl close to my back and an instant afterward the heavy thud of an animal that had jumped over the pickets and landed in the yard. It seemed only another instant before the two pups yelping and barking furiously had thrown themselves on the unwelcome visitor. I knew instinctively that the animal was a panther.

The struggling animals worked around to the front. The door was stoutly built but was fastened by a frail home-made wooden latch. I was terribly startled when a heavy jar nearly threw the latch out of its socket. The panther must have hurled the pups against the door. I knew another blow like that would break the lock and precipitate the fighting animals into our midst.

The piercing yaps and howls of my good little pups were getting louder every moment. Not knowing what to do I slipped out of bed again and there right under the long window in the bright moonlight I saw the panther. I could have touched him with a broomstick had the window been open. His small mean head, turned toward me, seemed all mouth—far too small for his long body.

I clapped my hands to frighten the beast away. The pups, mistaking this for a signal, rushed out from under the house and hurled themselves on the panther again. It was all done so quickly that I hardly followed with my eyes. Little Laddie was hurled against the logs and another swift blow from that powerful forearm hurled little Fox after her pal. I thought my dear little dogs had been killed.

Furiously angry, without a thought of consequences, I caught up my little Ivers-Johnson thirty-two caliber pistol and rushed to the door and threw it open.

The same instant both pups sprang past me into the cabin, throwing me off my balance. Fortunately I righted myself as I struck the ground and whirled to face the panther coming full tilt after the pups. Possibly the sudden apparition in white halted the snarling animal for an instant. My instinct for self preservation made me jerk up the pistol and fire. The panther plunged backward. I fired a second shot at something dark in the tall grass. Weak and unnerved I tumbled into the cabin and banged the door behind me. I had only one thought—the protection of my bed. There I found my boy shivering under the covers. The other boy was out of sight too. Not a sound from either.

As I pulled the covers over my head I heard a long wailing cry. I clutched my boy's arm. A few moments later we heard another cry farther off. It was unmistakably the wail of an animal in misery.

"I hit him," I shivered.

"You bet you did?" shivered my boy.

In the morning we could not find the dead panther near the cabin and were afraid to venture farther in our search. But later in the day two men came down off the range and reported seeing the dead panther a little way up the trail.

The little gun had done the work. Was the panther crazed by hunger or just taking out a grudge against the pups? That question none could answer but the panther and he can't.